PRAYER
THE KEY TO SALVATION

PRAYER
THE KEY TO SALVATION

By

Father Michael Müller, C.SS.R.

Priest of the Congregation of the Most Holy Redeemer

> *"Amen, amen I say to you: If you ask the Father any thing in my name, he will give it you. Hitherto you have not asked any thing in my name. Ask, and you shall receive; that your joy may be full."*
> —John 16:23-24

TAN BOOKS AND PUBLISHERS, INC.
Rockford, Illinois 61105

Imprimatur: ✠ Martin John Spalding, D.D.
                Archbishop of Baltimore
                October 22, 1867

Re-typeset by TAN Books and Publishers, Inc.

Library of Congress Catalog Card No.: 85-52207

ISBN: 0-89555-287-6

TAN BOOKS AND PUBLISHERS, INC.
P.O. Box 424
Rockford, Illinois 61105
1985

PROTEST OF THE AUTHOR

In obedience to the decrees of Urban VIII, of holy memory, I protest that I do not intend to attribute any other than purely human authority to all the miracles, revelations, graces, and incidents contained in this book; neither to the titles "holy" or "blessed," applied to the servants of God not yet canonized, except in cases where these have been confirmed by the Holy Roman Catholic Church, and by the Holy Apostolic See, of whom I profess myself an obedient son. And, therefore, to their judgment I submit myself and whatever I have written in this book.

CONTENTS

OBLATION

My Lord Jesus Christ, behold, I offer Thee this little work in union with that unspeakable charity which moved Thee to say: "Whatsoever you ask the Father in my name, that will I do: that the Father may be glorified in the Son. If you ask me any thing in my name, that I will do." (*John* 14:13-14). I offer this book to Thee on the part of all Thy creatures, because it is Thine ineffable tenderness for them which caused Thee to make them so unlimited a promise, thereby to draw them to Thyself, and to unite them to Thee eternally. Take this book, I beseech Thee, into Thy Divine keeping, that it may glorify the Omnipotence of Thy Father, Thine own Infinite Wisdom, and the unspeakable love of the Holy Ghost. I offer it to Thee in fervent thanksgiving for all the graces which Thou hast bestowed or wilt bestow through this little work, even to the end of the world. Place it, I beseech Thee, upon Thy most merciful Heart, that every word contained therein may be penetrated with Thy Divine sweetness, and fertilized by the merits of Thy holy life and of Thy Five Wounds. Consecrate, by an everlasting benediction, all that is said therein, that it may promote the salvation of those who read it with humble devotion. Inspire them with an irresistible desire of giving themselves up to prayer, that thus may be accomplished that exceedingly great desire of Thine, of manifesting Thyself to them in all Thy eternal goodness and charity; take them, as it were, into Thy Divine Heart as into a safe harbor of salvation, and breathe into their souls Thy eternal Divine Life and Truth. And as I am an utterly vile and unworthy creature, I offer Thee, in satisfaction for all my deficiencies and omissions, my blindness and ignorance, Thy own sweetest Heart, ever full of Divine thanksgiving and eternal beatitude.

Dear Mother Mary, do you also pray to your Divine Son for all those who may read this little book.

Chapter 1

INTRODUCTION

"Evil communications corrupt good manners," is a proverb as old as human experience. Why is it that association with the great and good improves our manners and our morals? I meet a great and good man; I hold intercourse or communion with him, and am never after what I was before. I feel that a virtue has gone forth from him and entered into my life, so that I am not, and can never be again, the man I was before I met him. What is the explanation of this fact? How happens it that I am benefited by my intercourse with the good, and injured by the intercourse with the bad? How is it that one man is able to influence another, whether for good or for evil? What is the meaning of *influence* itself? Influence, inflowing, flowing in —what is this but the fact that our life is the joint product of subject and object? Man lives, and can live only by communion with that which is not himself. This must be said of every living dependent existence. Only God can live in, from, and by Himself alone, uninfluenced and unaffected by anything distinguishable from His own being. But man is not God, is not being in himself, is not complete being, and must find out of himself both his being and his completeness. He lives not in and from himself alone, but does and must live in and by the life of another.

Cut off man from all communion with external nature, and he dies, for he has no sustenance for his body, and he must starve; cut him off from all communion with moral nature, and he dies, starves, morally; cut him off from all moral communion with a life above his own, and he stagnates, and can make no progress. All this everybody knows and concedes. Then to elevate man, to give him a higher and nobler life, you must give him a higher and nobler object, a higher and nobler life with which to commune. To elevate his subjective life, you must elevate his objective life. From the object must flow into him a higher virtue, an elevating element.

To illustrate: What is the good of each being? It is that which makes the being better and more perfect. It is clear that inferior beings cannot make superior ones better and more perfect. Now the soul, being immortal, is superior to all earthly or perishable things. These, then, cannot make the soul better and more perfect, but rather worse than she is; for he who seeks what is worse than himself makes himself worse than he was before. Therefore, the good— the life of the soul—can be only that which is better and more excellent than the soul herself is. Now God alone is this Good—He being Supreme Goodness Itself. He who possesses God may be said to possess the goodness of all other things, for whatever goodness they possess they have from God. It follows, then, most clearly that the closer our union is with God, or the more intimate our relation to Him is in this life, the more contentment of mind and the greater happiness of soul shall we enjoy.

Now communion between God and man is possible, for like communes with like. Now man has in his own nature a likeness to God. Human reason is the likeness in man of the Divine reason, and hence nothing hinders intercommunion between the reason of God and the reason of man. Though Divine reason, as the object, is independent of the human, and does not live by communion with it, yet the human reason lives only by communion with the Divine, as in all cases the subject lives only by communion with the object, and not reciprocally the object by communion with the subject. By this communion the subject partakes of the object, the human reason of the Divine reason, which is infinite, absolute truth.

Human reason, then, to live, to be, and to remain enlightened, must be and remain in communion with the Divine reason—with God. The more intimate its communion with God is, the more it will be enlightened, happy, and contented. Now this happy communion between the human and Divine reason—between the soul and God— remains established as long as the human reason acknowledges its dependence on the Divine reason, or as long as man obeys God's will, considers God as his Supreme Lord and Good, and the only Source of all true happiness.

When God made man, He might, by an act of His will, have decreed that the human reason should forever obey Him by an unvarying fixed law, as the stars do.

But God has His complacency in the homage of our free will, and so He made us *free* men, and not puppets, that nod the head and bend the knee as the wires are pulled. The Holy Scripture says of everything made by God: "And God saw that it was good." Man alone did not receive this praise. Why? It is because man has it in his power to become bad; he is free to choose good or evil, to side with God or with the devil, to follow truth or falsehood—light or darkness—to embrace virtue or vice. It is from this twofold liberty that have risen, from the beginning of the world, two powers, two elements continually combating each other—the good and the bad—the followers and children of God, and the adherents and friends of the devil. St. Michael the Archangel, and

Lucifer, the prince of the apostate angels, combat each other in Heaven; Cain and Abel in the family of Adam; Isaac and Ismael in that of Abraham; Jacob and Esau in that of Isaac; Joseph and his brethren in the family of Jacob; Solomon and Absalom in that of David; St. Peter and Judas in the company of Our Lord Jesus Christ; the Apostles and the Roman emperors in the Church of Christ; orthodox faith, or the Catholic Church, and heresy and infidelity, in the kingdom of God on earth; the just and the wicked, in all places; in fact, where is that country, that city, that village, or that family, howsoever small it may be, where these two elements or powers are not found in opposition?

Now it is only the followers of God that enjoy true liberty and happiness. To have the power or liberty to choose evil—to pass over to the devil and enlist and serve under his standard—is no power or liberty at all; it is a mark of weakness and misery, not of perfection. To illustrate: God is Supreme Liberty, and can do all things, yet He cannot sin. To have the power of sinning implies the possibility of becoming a slave of sin. Now the more this power of sinning in a man is increased or lessened, the more is also increased or lessened this possibility of slavery.

To illustrate: Ask a man whose heart is set on earthly gain, ask him what he thinks of those who renounce all to follow Christ and purchase Heaven; ask him, I say, whether they do wisely? Certainly he will answer, "They do wisely." Ask him again why he himself does not do what he commends in others; he will answer, "It is because I cannot." "Why can you not?" "Because avarice will not let me." It is because he is not free; he is not master of himself, nor of what he possesses. If he is truly master of himself and of what he has, let him lay it out to his own advantage; let him exchange earthly for heavenly goods; if he cannot, let him confess that he is not his own master, but a slave to his money.

It is, then, quite certain that the greatness of our liberty is in proportion to the power which our will has to *will* and to *do* what God wishes us to do. But let it be remembered that the greater this power is, the greater is also the goodness and perfection of our will; and the greater the perfection of our will, the greater is also the perfection of all its good actions; for the goodness and merit of our actions is in proportion to the goodness of our will. To illustrate: A man who is hardened in sin offends God more grievously when he sins, than another who sins out of frailty, or from a sudden outburst of passion, because he sins by a will determined to evil, which is to sin against the Holy Ghost; so, in like manner, all those good actions which proceed from a will quite determined to what is good, are doubtless of far greater perfection and merit than any others can be. The greater the artist, the more valuable is his work. So, before God, the better the will, the better and more meritorious are all its good actions.

A soul earnestly endeavoring to practice perfect obedience to the Divine will becomes, by degrees, so united with God as not to be able to will except what God wills; but not to be able to will except what God wills, is, as it were, to be what God is, with whom *to will* and *to be* is but one and the same thing; for to whomsoever power is given to become a child of God, to him is also given power, not indeed to be God Himself, but to be what God is.

To a soul thus disposed, the Lord grants such great favors as it is impossible to describe. He gives her a faith so lively, a confidence so firm, a charity so ardent, a zeal for the salvation of her neighbor so burning, a degree of prayer so sublime, a prudence so unusual, a courage in all difficulties so invincible, a peace so profound, a humility and simplicity of heart so admirable, and sometimes even a spirit so prophetic, together with a gift of performing miracles so extraordinary as to make everyone exclaim: "Truly, that soul can say with St. Paul, 'I live, now not I, but Christ liveth in me.'" (*Gal.* 2:20).

It was for his obedience to the will of God that Abel obtained from the Lord the testimony that he was just; that Henoch was translated by God, in order that he should not see death. On account of his obedience to the will of God, Noah and his family were saved from the deluge; Abraham became the father of many nations; Joseph was raised to the highest dignity at the court of the King of Egypt. Moses became the great servant, prophet, and lawgiver of the land, and the great performer of miracles with the people of God. Obedience to the will of God was, for the Jews, at all times, an impregnable rampart against all their enemies; it turned a Saul, a persecutor of the Church, into a Paul, the Apostle of the Gentiles; it turned the early Christians into martyrs, for martyrdom does not consist in suffering and dying for the Faith; it consists, rather, in the conformity of the martyr's will to the Divine will, which requires such a kind of death and not another.

On the contrary, disobedience turned the rebellious angels out of Heaven; it turned our first parents, Adam and Eve, out of Paradise; it made Cain a vagabond and a fugitive on earth; it drowned the human race in the waters of the deluge; it burned up the inhabitants of Sodom and Gomorrha. Disobedience to the will of God led the Jews often into captivity; it drowned Pharaoh and all his host in the Red Sea; it turned Nabuchodonosor into a wild beast, it laid the city of Jerusalem in ashes; it has ruined, and will still ruin, whole nations, empires, and kingdoms; it will finally put an end to the world, when all those who always rebelled against the will of God will, in an instant, be hurled into the everlasting flames of Hell, by these irresistible words of the Almighty: "Depart from me, ye cursed, into everlasting fire, which was prepared for the devil and his angels," there to obey the laws of God's justice forever. Man, then, when in opposition to God's will, is altogether out of his place. A tool which no longer corresponds to the end for which it was made is cast away; a wheel in a machinery which prevents others from working is taken out and replaced by another; a limb in the body which becomes burdensome and endangers the functions and life of the others, is cut off and thrown away; a servant who does no longer his master's will is discharged; a rebellious citizen, violating the laws of the state, is put into prison; a child, in an unreasonable opposition to his parents, is disinherited. Thus men naturally hate and reject what is unreasonable or useless, or opposed to, and destructive of, good order, whether natural or moral. What more natural, then, than that the Lord of Heaven and earth, the Author of good sense and of good order, should bear an implacable hatred to disobedience to His holy will?

The man in opposition to the will of God suffers as many pangs as a limb which has been dislocated; he is continually tormented by evil spirits, who have power over a soul that is out of its proper sphere of action; he is no longer under the protection of God, since he has withdrawn from His will, the rule for man's guidance, and has voluntarily left His watchful Providence. God sent Jonah, the prophet, to Nineveh, and he wished to go to Tarsus. He was buffeted by the tempest, cast into the sea, and swallowed by a monster of the deep! Behold what shall come on those who abandon God's will to follow their own passions and inclinations. They shall be tossed, like Jonah, by continual tempests; they will remain like one in a lethargy, in the hold of their vessels, unconscious of sickness or danger, until they perish in the stormy sea, and are swallowed up in Hell! "Know thou, and see that it is a bitter and fearful thing for thee to have left the Lord thy

God, when He desired to lead thee in the way of salvation, and that My fear is not with thee, saith the Lord God of Hosts."

God grants to the devil great power over the disobedient. As the Lord permitted a lion to kill a prophet in Juda in punishment for his disobedience to the voice of the Lord, so, in the same manner, He permits the infernal lion to assail the proud and the disobedient, everywhere, with the most filthy temptations, which they feel themselves too weak to resist, and thus fall a prey to his rage. Unless they repent soon, like Jonas, of their sin of idolatry, as it were, they will not be saved, as was the prophet, but will perish in the waves of temptations, and sink into the fathomless abyss of Hell.

Now why is it that many are good, and others are bad; that many follow God, and are saved, and others do not follow Him, and are damned? The answer to this question will be found in the following pages.

Chapter 2

ON THE NECESSITY OF
PRAYER IN GENERAL

There is an important truth of which thousands of men are ignorant; or if they know it, they reflect upon it seldom, and with but little fruit. Yet the knowledge of this truth is almost as necessary for all those who have attained the age of reason, as the knowledge of the mysteries of the Trinity and Incarnation. The importance of this great truth seems to be a mystery not merely to the heathen, Jews and heretics, but even to the greater part of Christians; nay, even to many of those who have consecrated themselves to God. We often hear in sermons, and read in pious books, of the necessity of avoiding bad company, of hating sin, of forgiving injuries, and of being reconciled to our enemies; but seldom are we taught this great truth, or, if it is sometimes spoken of, it is rarely done in a manner calculated to leave upon our minds a lasting impression of its great importance and necessity. Now this important truth is, that according to the ordinary course of Divine providence, man cannot be saved without prayer.

In order to understand this truth in its full extent, we must consider:

First. That we cannot be saved unless we fulfill the will of God.

Secondly. That we are unable to do God's will unless we are assisted by Divine grace.

Thirdly. That we obtain this grace by prayer alone; that consequently we must pray in order to be saved.

First. I say we cannot be saved unless we fulfill the will of God. The Lord declared His will in express terms when He said to Adam: "And of the tree of knowledge of good and evil thou shalt not eat; for in what day soever thou shalt eat of it, thou shalt die the death." (*Gen.* 2:17).

By this commandment man was clearly given to understand that the continuation of his happiness, for time and eternity, depended upon his obedience to the will of God. To be free from irregular affections and disorderly passions, and to transmit his happiness to his posterity, was entirely in his power. If he made a right use of his liberty, by always following the law of God; if he preserved unsullied the image and likeness of his Creator and heavenly Father; if, in fine, he made a proper use of the creatures confided to his care, he would then receive the crown of life everlasting in reward for his fidelity. But if he swerved even for a moment from this loving will of God, he would subject himself to the law of God's justice, which would not fail to execute the threatened punishment.

But did God, perhaps, afterwards, in consideration of the abundant merits of the Redemption, lay down other and easier conditions for man's happiness and salvation? No. He did not change these conditions in the least. Man's happiness still depended on his obedience to the Divine will. "Now if thou wilt hear the voice of the Lord thy God, to do and keep all his commandments, the Lord thy God will make thee higher than all the nations of the earth, and all these blessings shall come unto thee and overtake thee, yet so if thou hear his precepts." (*Deut.* 28:1-2). And our Divine Saviour says: "You are my friends, if you do the things that I command you." (*John*

15:14). And again: "Not every one that saith to me Lord, Lord, shall enter into the kingdom of heaven, but he that doth the will of my Father who is in heaven shall enter the kingdom of heaven." (*Matt.* 7:21). He Himself gave the example, having been obedient even unto the death of the Cross, thereby teaching all men that their salvation depends on their persevering obedience to the will of their heavenly Father.

Jesus Christ, the Redeemer, appointed the Apostles, and especially Peter, to succeed Him in His office of teaching the will of God. Where Peter and the other Apostles are found in their lawful successors, there only is the true and entire will of God taught; and those only who embrace and follow it faithfully, have well-founded hopes of salvation. They who follow any other rule in acquiring salvation deceive themselves. Instead of God's will, they do their own, or they follow the suggestions of the devil, or those of evil-minded, perverse teachers, who substitute their own will and opinions for the will of God; they imitate Adam and Eve, who believed the devil's suggestions rather than the infallible word of God.

But to be always mindful of God's will; always to honor, appreciate and love it above all things, always to embrace and follow it punctually and promptly; always to understand clearly, that whatever is contrary to God's will can never be good or meritorious, but must bring death to the soul; to return to His Divine will after having strayed away from it—all this is not the work of our weak nature, but is entirely the effect of Divine grace; for, if faith teaches us that God made all things very good, it also teaches us that they cannot remain so without God's assistance; otherwise they would cease to be dependent on Him. This is true of all God's creatures, but especially of man who, being endowed with free will, has it in his power to obey or transgress the law of God.

On this account Jesus Christ says: "Without Me you can do nothing." On these words, St. Augustine remarks that Jesus Christ did not say: "Without Me you cannot bring anything to perfection"; but He said: "You cannot even do anything." He means to say that without His grace we are not even able to commence any good work. "If this light of faith," said Our Lord to St. Catherine of Siena, "shineth on thee, thou wilt understand that I, thy God, know better how to promote thy welfare, and that I have a greater desire to do so than thou thyself, and that thou, without My grace, *neither wouldst nor couldst promote it."*

This very thing is taught by St. Paul. In his Second Epistle to the Corinthians he writes thus: "Not that we are sufficient to think anything of ourselves, as of ourselves, but our sufficiency is from God." (*2 Cor.* 3:5). The Apostle means to say that of ourselves we are not even able to think of any good or meritorious thing. Now, if we are not able to think of anything good, how much less able are we to wish for anything good. "It is God," he writes, in his Epistle to the Philippians, "who worketh in you, both to will and to accomplish, according to his good will." (*Phil.* 2:13).

The same thing had been declared by God long before, through the mouth of the prophet Ezechiel: "*I will cause you* to walk in my commandments, and keep my judgments and do them." (*Ezech.* 36:27).

Consequently, according to the teachings of St. Leo I, man works only so much good as God, in His grace, enables him to do. Hence it is an article of our holy faith that no one can do the least meritorious work without God's particular assistance.

But shall we, then, say that our first parents could not help losing the grace of God, and the many natural and supernatural gifts which they had received? Shall we say that when we sin, the fault lies not so much in us as in

God, who neglects to assist us? No! By no means; such an assertion would be a blasphemy. It is therefore certain:

1. That man is good in the sight of God, and has well-grounded hopes of salvation, only in proportion as he lives up to the will of God.

2. That man cannot, by his own strength, keep his will good, so as always to follow God's will under all circumstances.

3. That God must therefore have given man an infallible means, by the use of which he can preserve his innocence, and by the neglect of which he will certainly fall into sin.

The use of this means must be considered as an essential truth in the way of salvation. Our reason tells us that we should call upon the assistance of another, when we are unable to help ourselves. Adam and Eve knew this truth very well; but neglecting to call upon God's assistance in the hour of temptation, they lacked the grace necessary to enable them to keep the commandments of God. Hence they fell through their own fault.

We may, therefore, fairly conclude that the whole mystery of man's salvation and sanctification depends entirely on the constant and proper use of this great means of prayer. "As God, in the natural order," says St. Alphonsus, "ordained that man should be born naked, and in want of many of the necessaries of life, and as at the same time He has given him hands and understanding to provide for all his wants, so also in the supernatural order man is born incapable of remaining good, and obtaining salvation by his own strength; but God, in His infinite goodness, grants to everyone the grace of prayer, and wishes that all should make constant use of this grace, in order thereby to obtain all other necessary graces."

Prayer is a universal and infallible means of maintaining our relations with God. These relations are manifold.

The first is our dependence on God's goodness. By prayer, we acknowledge our dependence on God. As the subjects of a king acknowledge their dependence on their sovereign by paying the taxes he lays upon them, so also, by offering up to the Almighty the tribute of our prayer, we acknowledge ourselves to be constant mendicants before the gate of His Divine mercy.

The second relation by which we are united to God is faith. In this life we do not see God face to face; yet we must not, on that account, believe in Him less firmly. By prayer, we profess our faith in a God who knows, who is able and willing to grant all that we ask of Him.

The third relation is hope. We should hope that God will supply all our wants in this life, and grant us eternal happiness hereafter. What often troubles and disquiets so many souls is the uncertainty of their salvation; but according to the Apostle, our hope of salvation ought to be secure and immovable; and it will be so, undoubtedly, if it rests upon the solid foundations of *prayer* and the *promise of God*.

The power and mercy of God are indeed solid motives for hope, but the most solid is God's fidelity to His promises. God has promised, through the merits of Jesus Christ, to save us, and give us the graces necessary for our salvation. It is this promise which is the strongest of all motives of our hope of salvation because, though we believe that God is infinite in power and mercy, nevertheless, as Juvenino well observes, we could not have the unwavering certainty that God would save us, unless He Himself had given us the certain promise to do so.

But this infallible promise of God will avail us nothing unless we pray. Prayer is, then, the second solid foundation of our hope. Now as God has made us the infallible promise to give us all the graces we need, if we only pray for them, and as God has given the grace of prayer to everyone, no one can reasonably fear to be lost, if he really perseveres in prayer. We can therefore truly say with St. Alphonsus: "I never feel more confident of my salvation than when I pray." This is evident. The more often we converse with a true and virtuous friend, the better do we become acquainted with his good qualities; and the more we know his good qualities, the greater will be our confidence that he will keep the promises he has made us. Now as prayer is a conversation with God, the more often we pray, the better do we learn to know God; for it is especially in prayer that God reveals Himself to the soul. Now the more we know God, the greater is our confidence that He will keep the promises which He has made us, through the merits of His Divine Son. Thus prayer is truly the mother and nurse of hope.

The fourth relation is charity. By prayer we preserve and increase the Divine virtue of charity. Prayer brings us nearer to God; It is like the magnetic fluid which passes over the telegraph wire from one operator to another. By means of this fluid they can communicate with each other at the very same moment; they are thus brought in close proximity to each other, though they may be in reality far apart. Now prayer brings us nearer to God than the magnetic fluid does two telegraph operators. By means of prayer we make known to God all our desires and all our necessities, spiritual and temporal; and while we are praying, all the gifts and treasures of God's bounty descend upon our souls. Who can doubt that by this close intercourse of the soul with God, the fire of Divine love will be enkindled and increased in a most wonderful manner.

The fifth relation between God and the soul is that of a father to his child. Now God, as Father, has an unspeakable desire to communicate His benefits to us. "My delights were to be with the children of men." (*Prov.* 8:31). It is in prayer that God makes known to us His ineffable sweetness, and communicates to us the gifts of His inexhaustible treasures. This infinite desire of God, to bestow upon us the riches of His Divinity, will manifest itself superabundantly in Heaven.

In this life we must merit eternal happiness by faithfully observing the law of God; but, at the same time, eternal happiness remains always a free gift of God. "What hast thou, that thou hast not received? And if thou hast received, why dost thou glory as if thou hadst not received?" (*1 Cor.* 4:7). Thus we are always dependent on God for the grace of final perseverance. Now by prayer we are enabled to correspond with the grace of God, and can thus merit eternal life.

O, admirable wisdom of God, which has established for man's salvation and sanctification so easy and so infallible a means as that of prayer! What can be more important for man than the faithful fulfillment of this duty of prayer? And yet, strange to say, there is nothing less understood and less attended to than this very duty! The neglect and careless performance of this duty of prayer have ever been the fruitful source of all moral evils, and even of infidelity and idolatry. The more we neglect to pray to God, the true Life of our soul, the more we shall experience the weakness of our will to resist vice and sin. Our passions, the temptations of the devil, and the allurements of the world will draw us headlong from one abyss of wickedness to another.

When in imminent danger of death, or of a considerable loss of fortune, as, for instance, in case of a shipwreck, or fire, or the like, the greater part of men will, indeed, remember their duty of praying to God as the only one who can save them from death. On such occasions even infidels will lay aside the mask of infidelity and make a profession of faith in an Almighty God, crying out: "Lord save us, we are perishing! Lord have mercy on us!" Except on such occasions, the greater part of men do not care for prayer. Would to God they loved their souls as much as their bodies, and the perishable goods of this world! Would to God they understood the danger in which they are of being condemned to the everlasting pains of Hell! They would then, indeed, feel naturally compelled to pray to the Almighty for the grace of salvation.

But, alas! Men love their evil ways more than the practice of prayer. In almost every page of Holy Writ God exhorts us to observe His commandments. In like manner He continually urges us to pray, for it is by prayer that we are enabled to keep His commandments. God speaks of the obligation of prayer in the clearest language, on almost every page of Holy Scripture. "Seek ye the Lord," He says by the Royal Prophet, "and be strengthened: seek his face evermore." (*Ps.* 104:4). "Let nothing keep thee from praying always." (*Ecclus.* 18:22).

What God inculcated so clearly in the Old Law is still more clearly and more forcibly inculcated by Jesus Christ in the New Law. "And he spoke a parable to them, that we ought always to pray, and not to faint." (*Luke* 18:1). And again: "Watch ye and pray." (*Matt.* 26:41).

This precept to pray always and not to faint was also taught and emphatically inculcated in His name by the Apostles. "But we will give ourselves continually to prayer," says St. Peter. (*Acts* 6:4). "By all prayer and supplication," writes St. Paul to the Ephesians, "praying at all times in the spirit; and in the same watching with all instance and supplication for all the saints." (*Eph.* 6:18). And again: "Be instant in prayer, watching in it in thanksgiving." And to the Thessalonians he writes: "Pray without ceasing." (*1 Thess.* 5:17). And to his beloved disciple Timothy he writes: "I will, therefore, that men pray in every place, lifting up pure hands without anger and contention." (*1 Tim.* 2:8).

Can the necessity of prayer be more clearly and more forcibly expressed than it is in these passages of Holy Scripture? It is not said anywhere that it is good to pray, that it is advisable or that it is useful to pray; no! It is said in the clearest language, "*You* must *pray*." It is not said: "You must pray *now* and *then*"; no! It is said: "You must pray *always*"; "You must pray *without ceasing*"; "You must not *faint in prayer*"; "You must *watch in it* at *all times* and in *all places*." All these expressions imply, according to all the theologians of the Church, a formal precept of prayer, so that, in their opinion, a man who would not pray for a month could not be excused from mortal sin.

Had we, then, no other evidence of the necessity of prayer than the fact that Jesus Christ and His Apostles have always inculcated it so earnestly, this fact alone should be sufficient to convince us of its necessity; for just as we firmly believe that there are three Persons in God, simply because Jesus Christ has taught us this truth, so, in like manner, ought we to be firmly convinced of the necessity of prayer, for the simple reason that Jesus Christ Himself has taught it in the clearest language; for being Truth Itself, He could never have taught us anything as necessary which was not really so.

But as there is no more persuasive way of instruction than example, Our Lord Jesus Christ taught us the necessity of prayer by His Divine example, even before He taught it by His word. Is it not strange, indeed, to behold the Son of God, Eternal Wisdom Itself, who came into this world to teach men the way of salvation, who, in His childhood, might have preached and wrought miracles for the conversion of sinners, just as easily as He did at the age of thirty years; is it not strange, I say, to see Him spend thirty years in retirement and obscurity, unknown to the world, and losing, according to our manner of judging,

His most precious time?

Now God is Infinite Wisdom, and always acts reason-ably. Why, then, did He act in this strange manner? It was in order to give us an example which we should imitate. During those thirty years, the Son of God was not idle; He spent His time in the practice of virtue and in continual prayer.

Now the Son of God does not need to pray for Himself. He prayed in order to teach us, by His Divine example, the absolute necessity of prayer. Thirty years of His life were consecrated to this holy exercise, and three years only to the instruction of the people, and even of this short period of three years He spent the greater part in prayer. How often did He not say to His disciples: "Withdraw a little from the multitude"? And for what purpose? In order to be more at liberty to pray. Moreover, do we not read in the Gospel that, after having spent the day in instructing the people, He would retire to a lonely mountain, there to spend the whole night in prayer? "And it came to pass that he went out into a mountain to pray, and he passed the whole night in prayer to God." (*Luke* 6:12). This was a custom of our Saviour, as we may gather from the fact that Judas, the traitor, did not go with the soldiers to seek Him in the city of Jerusalem, but went straightway to the Mount of Olives, because he knew that Jesus was ac-customed to go thither to spend the night in prayer.

Again, wishing to be glorified by His heavenly Father, He prayed for it. And lifting up His eyes to Heaven, He said: "Father, the hour is come; glorify thy Son." (*John* 17:1). On this prayer, Father Crasset, S. J., remarks: "Jesus prays His Father to glorify His body. Now was not this His due?" Had He not merited it? Could His Father refuse Him? Why, then, did He ask it? It is because God had decreed not to grant any favor to man, not even to His Divine Son, except through prayer, which is the channel through which all graces flow. "Ask, My Son," saith He, "for all the nations of the earth, and I will give them to Thee for Thy inheritance." Jesus merited the empire of the whole universe, and yet He obtained it only after asking for it.

"Even in Heaven," as St. Paul assures us, "He is continually interceding for us." He has been doing this for more than eighteen hundred years, and He will continue to do so to the end of the world.

He likewise intercedes for us in the Sacrifice of the Mass; for Mass, according to the doctrine of the Catholic Church, is a sacrifice of impetration, in which Jesus Christ asks of His heavenly Father everything necessary for our spiritual and temporal welfare. Now, if we consider that Mass is said at every hour of the day, it follows that Jesus Christ, for more than eighteen hundred years, has been continually praying for us under the Sacramental Species, and that He will continue to do so at every hour until the end of the world.

Truly, if this example of our Saviour does not convince us of the necessity of prayer, it will be in vain to look for other and more striking proofs in confirmation of this truth. "Jesus Christ," remarks St. Augustine, "is the Lord of Heaven and earth; He is happy in Himself and in need of nothing, and yet He prays; shall, then, man, who is misery itself, not pray? Jesus Christ, our Divine Physician, lies prostrate in prayer—and shall we, who are sick in body and soul, think it too much to kneel down to pray? Jesus Christ is Innocence Itself, and yet He prays; we are laden with sin, and shall we not pray? Jesus Christ, the Judge of the living and the dead, prays, and shall we not pray who are so guilty in His sight?"

St. Augustine wishes to say that Jesus Christ came into this world to instruct us both by His words and example: "I have given you an example, that, as I have done, so do you also." (*John* 13:15). Now to disregard this Divine example is to forsake the order of God's goodness, in order to fall into that of His justice; it is to renounce His friendship, in order to incur His just anger. To neglect to follow Our Lord's example, is to stray away on dangerous paths; it is to turn all our pleasures into bitterness; it is to bring all our plans to naught; it is to make all our labors useless; it is to make even our very prosperity a chastisement; it is to make our trials and afflictions a source of despair, and our very existence a Hell.

On the contrary, to follow this example is to place ourselves in perpetual peace and security; it is to oblige the wisdom of God to govern us, His power to defend us, His goodness to console us, His grace to sanctify us, His mercy to encompass us, His sanctity to purify us, His providence to preserve us from evil and to sustain us in good, and to make all go well with us in time and in eternity.

Chapter 3

ON THE NECESSITY OF
PRAYER FOR SINNERS

I have dwelt long on the necessity of prayer in general.
Now it may seem useless to prove the necessity of prayer
for sinners, or for the just in particular. But the truth I
treat of is of the most vital importance in the way of salvation and sanctification. The more clearly it is understood,
the better it will be practiced, and our hope for salvation
increases in proportion to our love for prayer.

Jesus Christ, speaking of the just, says: "As the branch
cannot bear fruit of itself, unless it abide in the vine, so
neither can you, unless you abide in me." (*John* 15:4).
Now if this be true of those who already enjoy the grace of
God, it is especially true of sinners. The poor sinner,
deprived of God's grace, is like a child who is helpless and
abandoned. He is unable, of his own strength, to rise from
the state of sin and recover the friendship of God. "If anyone," says the Council of Trent, "asserts that without the
preceding inspiration and grace of the Holy Ghost man
can believe, hope, love, or repent in such a manner as he
ought, let him be anathema." Consider well the word:
"Repent in such a manner as he ought." Judas, too, repented, for Holy Scripture says of him: "Then Judas, who
betrayed Jesus, seeing that he was condemned, repenting

22

himself, brought back the thirty pieces of silver to the chief priests and ancients, saying: I have sinned in betraying innocent blood." (*Matt.* 27:3). But this was not such repentance as is required for justification; it proceeded only from natural motives, and consequently led to despair. "And Judas," as Holy Scripture says, "went and hanged himself with a halter." (*Matt.* 27:5). We can indeed fall into sin without any assistance; but rise from sin we cannot, except by the special assistance of God. I can pluck out my eyes, but to set them in again properly is beyond my power. I can likewise lose the grace of God, but to recover it again without God's assistance, is more than I can do. St. Peter remained chained in prison until an angel came and said to him, "Arise," and the chains fell off from his hands. (*Acts* 12:7). Had St. Peter not been awakened by the angel, he would not have thought of rising; and should he have thought of it, he would not have been able to free himself from his fetters. In like manner, the soul which has once been chained by sin will scarcely ever think seriously of being converted, and returning to God; and should it ever think of this, all its efforts will not suffice to break the chains of sin, and free it from the slavery of the devil, if God's grace does not come to its aid.

One day St. Anselm met a boy playing with a bird. The poor bird tried to fly away, but it could not, as the boy held it by a thread which he had tied to its leg. The little bird tried to fly away again and again, but the boy always pulled it back, and laughed and leaped for joy, as he saw it flutter and fall upon the ground. St. Anselm stood gazing for a considerable time at this strange sport, and showed the greatest compassion for the poor little bird. Suddenly the thread broke, and the little bird flew away. The boy began to cry, but St. Anselm expressed the greatest joy. All present were astonished to see so great a prelate take such interest in this childish sport. But St. Anselm said: "Do you know what I thought of on seeing this boy amuse himself thus with the bird? Ah! It is thus, thought I, that the devil makes sport of sinners. He ties them at first, as it were, with a slender thread, and then sports with them as he pleases, drawing them from one sin to another." Some he ties by indifference to God and to their own salvation, others by too great love for the good of this world; some, again, he ties by the sin of avarice, others by the sin of uncleanness, others by the sin of theft, and so on. Many a one of the unfortunate sinners, seeing his great misery, will cry and sigh like St. Augustine: "How long, O Lord! Wilt Thou be angry forever? Remember not my past iniquities." And perceiving himself still held back by them, he cast forth miserable complaints, and reproached himself, saying: "How long? How long? Tomorrow! Tomorrow! Why not now? Why does not this hour put an end to my filthiness?" These complaints he uttered, and he wept with most bitter contrition of heart, not feeling courage enough to renounce his evil ways.

"Oh! Would to God," cries many a sinner, "that I were free from this accursed habit of drinking, of swearing, of sinning against the angelic virtue of holy purity! What am I to do?" Like the little bird, this poor sinner wishes to get free from his sinful habits, but in vain. The devil keeps him tied by his evil habits, and drags him back into his old sins. At last the unhappy wretch, seeing that he cannot get free, gives way to despair.

Many sinners even become so hardened that they resemble incarnate demons—even were Hell open before them, they would still continue to sin. Others, again, are so unhappy that they do not see their misery, and some even do not wish to see it, lest they should feel any stings of conscience, and conceive a desire of amendment.

There are others who would indeed wish to amend, and

even feel the good will to do so, but they lack courage and energy.

Oh, unhappy state of sinners! Whence shall such men obtain light to understand their misery? Whence shall they receive the good will, the courage and energy to free themselves from their evil habits? It is from God alone; He can grant these graces. "The heart of man," says Holy Writ, "is in the hand of the Lord; He turns it whithersoever He wills." God can in one moment enlighten the sinner so that he understands the misery and danger of his state. The Lord can so move his will, that he makes a firm resolution to amend. He can in one moment inspire the heart of the sinner with so much confidence in His mercy, that he firmly hopes for the forgiveness of all his sins.

But on what condition does God grant these all-important graces? He grants them only on condition that the sinner prays for them. The Lord is always ready to receive the sinner again into His friendship, provided he sincerely desires it. He has solemnly declared by the mouth of His prophet: "As I live, saith the Lord, I wish not for the death of the sinner, but that he be converted and live." (*Ezech.* 33:11).

The Lacaedemonians, in order to make their children expert in the use of the bow, were accustomed to place their food in a position beyond their reach, and they then said: "Now, children, there is your food; shoot it down, if you want it." It is thus that God seems to speak to sinners. "Behold," He says, "poor helpless sinners, My grace is ready for you at any time. Aim at it, that is, pray to Me for it, if you want it; for as many graces will descend upon you as you will shoot down by the darts of prayer; and should you not even have the desire to pray for My grace, or should you have no fervor in prayer, then ask for the grace to pray with all earnestness and fervor, and be assured this grace shall be given you; if you neglect to do so, you shall certainly perish. I told you often, and I repeat it again: 'Call on me, and I will hear you'; 'Ask, and you shall receive' (*John* 16:23); 'Whatsoever you ask, you shall receive.' (*Matt.* 21:22).

"And lest anyone should suppose that this promise applied only to the just, I have added purposely: 'Everyone who asks shall receive.' (*Matt.* 7:7). Everyone, without exception, whether he be a just man or a sinner, shall receive what he asks of Me, but ask he must." Thus God, in His infinite goodness, has promised to give everything to him who prays.

Prayer, therefore, is a universal means by which every single grace necessary to bring us *infallibly* to eternal life may be obtained with infallible certainty, since the Son of God cannot be a liar. In this respect it differs from the Sacraments, from penitential works, and the other means which God has given us in order to obtain eternal life. These are particular means, each producing or procuring particular graces; Baptism produces one grace, and Penance another; it is the same for the other Sacraments or means of salvation. But to none of these, nor to all put together, without prayer, has God promised all the graces necessary for eternal life. Prayer is the only means to which He has promised all the *efficacious* helps and graces necessary for our salvation. It is a means given to all, without exception; for God gives the grace of prayer to the most hardened sinners as well as to the most holy of the just; and He has given it to every adult that ever lived, from the time of Adam to the present day. By making a good use of this grace of prayer, the worst sinner may obtain, as *infallibly* as the greatest saint, every efficacious grace necessary for his salvation, and may thus *infallibly* secure everlasting glory, for Jesus Christ has promised to hear the prayers of all—of sinners as well as saints: "For everyone that asketh, receiveth." (*Luke* 11:10). He who says everyone, excepts none.

Hence St. Alphonsus says: "One of the greatest pains of the damned is the thought that they could have saved themselves so easily by asking of God to give them true sorrow for their sins, and a firm will to amend their lives. No one, therefore," says the saint, "can excuse himself before God by saying that his salvation was impossible, on account of the difficulties and obstacles which he met in the way of salvation. God will not hearken to such an excuse; He will answer: 'If you had not strength and courage enough to overcome all obstacles and difficulties in the way of your salvation, why did you not ask Me to come to your assistance?' If a man has fallen into a deep pit, and will not take hold of the rope that is let down to draw him up, it is clearly his own fault if he perishes. Thus the sinner, too, is lost through his own fault, if he neglects to pray for his salvation. 'I have waited for you so many years,' the Lord will say to the sinner, 'in the hope that you would at last ask for the grace of true repentance, and for the amendment of your sinful life. Had you only asked, you would have instantly received; for to call on Me for assistance is to be delivered and saved.'"

Chlodwig (Clovis), heathen king of the Franks, when, with his whole army, in imminent danger of being defeated by the Alemanni, prayed as follows:

"Jesus Christ, Thou of Whom Chlotilde (the king's Christian wife) has often told me that Thou art the Son of the living God, and that Thou givest aid to the hard pressed and victory to those who trust in Thee, I humbly crave Thy powerful assistance. If Thou grantest me the victory over my enemies, I will believe in Thee and be baptized in Thy name. For I have called upon my gods in vain. They must be impotent, as they cannot help those who serve them. Now I invoke Thee, desiring to believe in Thee; do, then, deliver me from the hands of my adversaries."

No sooner had Chlodwig uttered this prayer than the Alemanni became panic-stricken, took to flight, and soon after, seeing their king slain, sued for peace. Thereupon Chlodwig blended both nations, the Franks and the Alemanni, together—returned home, and became a Christian. Should any one of my readers be still groping in the darkness of unbelief or error, I would kindly request him to pray in the same spirit, adapting King Chlodwig's prayer to his own circumstances; or to say the prayer which F. Thayer, a minister of the Anglican Church, used to say when he was yet in doubt and uncertainty, and by which he obtained for himself the gift of faith. He prayed as follows:

"God of all goodness, Almighty and Eternal Father of mercies, and Saviour of mankind; I implore Thee, by Thy Sovereign goodness, to enlighten my mind and to touch my heart, that, by means of true faith, hope, and charity, I may live and die in the true religion of Jesus Christ. I confidently believe that, as there is but one God, there can be but one Faith, one religion, one only path to salvation, and that every other path opposed thereto can lead but to perdition. This path, O my God! I anxiously seek after, that I may follow it and be saved. Therefore I protest before Thy Divine Majesty, and I swear by all Thy Divine Attributes, that I will follow the religion which Thou shalt reveal to me as the true one, and will abandon, at whatever cost, that wherein I shall have discovered errors and falsehoods. I confess that I do not deserve this favor, for the greatness of my sins, for which I am truly penitent, seeing they offend a God Who is so good, so holy, and so worthy of love; but what I deserve not I hope to obtain from Thine Infinite Mercy; and I beseech Thee to grant it unto me through the merits of that precious Blood which was shed for us sinners by Thine only Son, Jesus Christ our Lord, Who liveth and reigneth, etc. Amen."

Indeed, fire does not burn tow more quickly than God enlightens and forgives sinners, when they ask His light and forgiveness. The woman of Cana had no sooner said, "Lord, help me!" than she was heard, and received the grace of conversion. The Samaritan woman, too, received the grace of conversion as soon as she asked Our Lord for the living water of which He had spoken to her. No sooner had the publican prayed in the temple, "Lord be merciful to me, a sinner!" than he was instantly forgiven, and left the temple justified. No sooner had the good thief on the cross said to our Saviour, "Lord, remember me when Thou comest into Thy Kingdom!" than he was forgiven, and even received the promise that he would be with Him that day in Paradise. Say daily the following ejaculation, that you may be saved:

"My Lord Jesus Christ, for the sake of Thy sufferings, grant me such faith, hope, charity, sorrow for my sins, and love for prayer, as will save and sanctify my soul."

Father Hunolt, S. J., relates that there was once a certain vicious young man who often sincerely wished to change his life, but who, on account of his deeply rooted evil habits, believed his conversion utterly impossible. He thought that whatever he might do would be of no avail to excite true sorrow and contrition in his heart. One day, overwhelmed with melancholy, he left home, in order to seek some relief in the society of his companions. On leaving the house he met, at the door, a poor beggar. As soon as he saw him, he remembered the words of Our Lord Jesus Christ: "Whatsoever you have done to the least of My brethren, you have done to Me." He then went and took a loaf of bread, and, throwing himself on his knees before the beggar, he gave it to him, thus praying in his heart: "My Lord Jesus Christ, I adore Thee in the person of this poor man! Most gladly would I give Thee my whole heart, but I cannot, because it is too hardened; for the present, at least, take, I beseech Thee, this loaf of bread, which I am still able to give; do with my heart whatever Thou wilt." Oh, the wonderful power of prayer! No sooner had he prayed thus, than he felt a most bitter sorrow for all his sins, and shed a torrent of tears. He made a good confession, and ever afterward received many extraordinary graces. (11th Sermon on the Following of Christ).

La Harpe was an infidel, and a great friend of Voltaire; he wrote several works against religion. At last, when the French Revolution broke out, he was seized and cast into prison. There, in the silence and solitude of his cell, he found time to examine the truths of religion, which he had hitherto neglected. He was, as he himself relates, sad and lonely in his cell. To while away his time, he read a few pious books that had been given him. Gradually the light of faith began to dawn again in his heart; but this heavenly light filled him with terror. All the sins of his whole life came up before him. He knew that death was at hand; for in those days, there was but one step from the prison to the scaffold. For the first time in forty years he turned to God in a humbled, sorrowful heart, and began *to pray.* There was no priest near to prepare him for death. They were all dead, banished, or put to death. What was he to do? At last, after having offered up *a fervent prayer,* he opened, at random, a copy of the *Imitation of Christ,* and read these consoling words: "See, my son, I have come to thee, because thou hast called Me." These words filled him with unspeakable consolation. His heart was touched; he fell upon his face; he burst into tears. This was the beginning of a new life. La Harpe was afterwards set free; but he remained ever after faithful to the good resolutions he had formed whilst shut up in his dreary prison.

Would to God that all those saints now in Heaven, who, for a while, led a sinful life on earth, could stand before you at this moment! Would that you could ask them in person: "Beloved souls, why did you not die in your sins? Why were you forgiven?" "Ah!" they would answer, "it was because we implored the Lord for mercy and forgiveness." "But how did it happen that you did not relapse into your former sins? How were you able to persevere in leading a penitential life until death?" "Beloved brethren," they would answer, "know that this good will, this strength and courage came not from ourselves; no, of ourselves we were too weak, like you; we were often tempted to commit the same sins again, but then we had recourse to prayer, and God assisted us, and preserved us from sin. Prayer makes the soul unconquerable. No evil spirit has the least power over her as long as she prays. It is, then, by prayer that we were enabled to give up sin, lead a penitential life, and to die as holy penitents."

Ah, would that some of the souls now burning in Hell could come forth and tell us why they were lost! What, think you, would the bad thief say, who was crucified at the same time with our Saviour? "Ah!" he would say, "I confess that I was a very wicked sinner throughout the course of my whole life; I committed many crimes, for which I have deserved Hell a thousand times; but my companion on the cross was not less guilty; his sins cried not less to Heaven for vengeance; yet he ascended from his cross into Heaven, whilst I, from mine, was hurled into the depth of Hell; he rejoices forever, while I am tormented in everlasting fire. What brought him into Heaven? It was the simple prayer: 'Lord, remember me when Thou comest into Thy kingdom.' What brought me to Hell? It was the neglect of prayer; because I would not pray I remained hardened in my sins, and died as a reprobate."

Dear reader, rest assured that all the damned would give the same answer were they allowed to tell us the cause of their damnation. O language full of terror to hardened sinners, who do not wish to give up their sinful lives and return to God! O language full of sweetness and consolation for all those who pray to be delivered from their sins, and to be received again as children of God!

Ah, would to God that I could stand on a high mountain, surrounded by all the sinners in the world! I would cry aloud, at the top of my voice: "Pray, pray, pray! You will not die in your sins; you will be forgiven; you will be saved, if you only pray! God does not require that you should go and sell everything and give it to the poor; or be put to the rack, or be nailed to a cross, in order to save your soul; conditions so painful as these He does not require of you; He requires the easiest in the world; all that He asks is that you should pray, and sincerely entreat Him to save you. He is still the same God; He is still as powerful to help you, just as merciful to forgive you, and to receive you again into His friendship, as He was when He said to the good thief: 'This day shalt thou be with Me in Paradise.'" He will be to you the same powerful, the same merciful God, that he was to St. Magdalen the Penitent, to St. Augustine, to St. Margaret of Cortona, to St. Mary of Egypt, and to many other souls whom He has delivered from their sins, and even changed into saints. But you must avail yourself of His promise: "Amen, amen I say unto you, whatever you ask the Father in my name, he shall give it to you." (*John* 16:23). Jesus Christ has made this promise, and He will never fail to keep it. "Heaven and earth will pass away, but His word shall never pass away." He alone is lost who does not pray; he alone will be saved who perseveres in prayer. On the Last Day, all the saints of Heaven, as well as also all the damned souls of Hell, will bear witness to this truth; on that great day you, too, will bear witness to it, either with the elect on the right, if you *have prayed during life,* or with the damned on the left, *if you have neglected to pray.* Choose now whichever lot you prefer, but choose in time.

Chapter 4

ON THE NECESSITY OF PRAYER FOR THE JUST

If a man knows that he has never deserved the good graces of his king, that the friendship which he enjoys is a pure gift, and that he is to possess it only as long as he continues to ask for it, would he not, in case he wished to enjoy it always, be obliged to entreat his benefactor to continue this favor? Now this is precisely the case with the just in regard to the friendship, the grace of God. The grace of God is a pure gift, which no one can obtain by his own efforts, and, when it is obtained, no one can preserve it until death, unless God assist him.

God is an Infinite God. To possess His grace is to possess God Himself. Now, to persevere in the possession of this grace until death is so great a favor, that, according to the teachings of the Fathers of the Church, no one can merit it, even were he to perform all the good works of all the saints in Heaven. God bestows this gift gratuitously; and He grants it, as St. Augustine teaches, to all those who daily pray for it. The saint says: "We must pray for it *every day,* because even the just are *every day* in danger of losing it."

It will be well to consider here this daily danger, as it will thoroughly convince us that the just stand in need of prayer. St. Paul the Apostle says: "He that striveth for the mastery is not crowned except he strive lawfully." (*2 Tim.* 2:5). By this he means that no one shall be crowned with life everlasting unless he fight manfully until death against his enemies, the devil, the world, and his own corrupt nature. In this warfare, the just are often in great danger of being overcome on account of the weakness of human nature, and the malice and subtlety of their enemies.

St. Peter says that "the devil goeth about as a roaring lion, seeking whom he may devour." (*1 Peter* 5:8). It was this archenemy that persuaded Adam and Eve to eat of the forbidden fruit; it was he that prevailed on Cain to slay his innocent brother Abel; it was he that tempted Saul to pierce David with a lance; it was he that stirred up the Jews to deny and crucify Jesus Christ, Our Lord; it was he that induced Ananias and Sapphira to lie to the Holy Ghost; it was he who urged Nero, Decius, Diocletian, Julian, and other heathen tyrants, to put the Christians to a most cruel death; it is he who inspired the authors of heresies, such as Arius, Martin Luther, and others, to reject the authority of the one true Catholic Church.

In like manner, the devil at the present day still tempts all men, especially the just, and endeavors to make them lose the grace of God. He tempts numberless souls to indifference toward God and their salvation; he deceives many by representing to them, in glowing colors, the false, degrading pleasures of this world; he suggests to others the desire of joining certain bad secret societies; he tempts many even to conceal their sins in confession, and to receive Holy Communion unworthily; others, again, he urges to cheat their neighbor; he allures others to blind their reason by excess in drinking; others, again, he tempts to despair; in a word, the devil leaves nothing untried in order to make the just fall into sin; he attacks everyone in his weak point; and the devil knows that this weak point is for many, very many, a strong inclination to the shameful vice of impurity. This wicked spirit knows how to excite in them this degrading passion to such a degree, that they forget all their good resolutions, nay, even make little account of the eternal truths, and lose all fear of Hell and the Divine Judgment. It is the universal opinion of all theologians that there are more souls condemned to Hell on account of this sin alone, than on account of any other which men commit.

But the just must not only wage war against their arch-enemy—the devil—they must also fight manfully against the seductive examples of the world. Were all those who have lost their baptismal innocence to tell us how they came to lose it, they would all answer: "It was by this corrupt companion, by this false friend, by this wicked relative. Had I never seen this wicked wretch, I would still be innocent." One unsound apple is sufficient to infect all the others in its neighborhood. In like manner one corrupt person can ruin all those with whom he associates. Indeed the bad example of one wicked man can do more harm to a community, than all the devils in Hell united. Small indeed is the number of those who manfully resist bad example.

There is still another truth to be considered here. St. Paul the Apostle says: "All that live godly in Christ Jesus shall suffer persecution." (*2 Tim.* 3:12). All those who endeavor to serve Our Lord Jesus Christ faithfully, and to persevere in His service, will have to suffer in some way or other from their fellow men. Sometimes they will have to suffer from jealous and envious neighbors; sometimes from bad comrades, whose company they have given up; sometimes, again, they are blamed, rashly judged, and condemned; and what is the most painful of all, God, to try their patience and charity, often permits them to suffer most from those very persons from whom they should naturally expect sympathy and consolation. Very small indeed is the number of those who, under such severe trials, remain faithful to God. The greater part, even of the just, cannot bear detraction and calumny. To suffer a temporal loss seems almost insupportable; to forgive an injury or an insult is more than they can do; they try to avoid those who have offended them; bitterly complain of them, and sometimes even curse them.

The just have to fight not only against the devil and the world, but also against their own corrupt nature. Had they not this enemy to contend with, the devil and the world would not so easily overcome them. Corrupt nature plays the traitor, and very often gains the victory over them, even when the two other enemies have failed. This dangerous enemy is always near, even within their very hearts. Even the greater number of the just do not seem to be fully aware of the power of this domestic enemy; hence it is that they are so little on their guard against his wiles, and fall a prey to his evil suggestions.

Ever since the fall of our first parents, we are all naturally inclined to evil. Before Adam had committed sin, he was naturally inclined to good; he knew nothing of indifference in the service of God, nothing of anger, hatred, cursing, impurity, vain ambition, and the like; but no sooner had he committed sin, than God permitted his inclination to good to be changed into an inclination to evil. Man of his own free will forfeited the kingdom of Heaven; he exchanged Heaven for Hell, God for the devil, good for evil, the state of grace for the state of sin. It was, then, but just and right that he should not only acknowledge his guilt, repent sincerely of his great crime, but should also, as long as he lived, fight against his evil inclinations, and, by this lifelong warfare, declare himself sincerely for God.

Baptism, indeed, cancels Original Sin in our soul, but it does not destroy our natural inclination to evil, which we have inherited from our first parents. The great Apostle St. Paul bears witness to this: "I do not that good which I will," he says, "but the evil which I hate, that I do." (*Rom.* 7:15). He means to say, I do not wish to do evil; I even try to avoid it; but I experience within myself a continual inclination to evil; I endeavor to do good, but I feel within myself a great reluctance thereto, and I must do violence to myself in order to act aright. Everyone has, from his childhood, experienced this evil inclination. We naturally feel more inclined to anger than to meekness; more inclined to disobedience than to submission; we are more prone to hatred than to love; more inclined to gratify the evil desires of our heart than to practice the holy virtue of purity; we prefer our own ease to visiting Jesus Christ in the Blessed Sacrament, or receiving Him in Holy Communion; we are naturally indifferent toward God and His holy religion; we lack fervor in His Divine service; we often feel more inclined to join a forbidden society than to enter a pious confraternity; we often find more pleasure in reading a bad or useless book than one that is good and edifying; we are more apt to listen to uncharitable and unbecoming conversation, than to the word of God; we feel naturally more inclined to vainglory, pride, and levity, than to humility, self-contempt, and the spirit of mortification.

When we consider seriously the continual war we have to wage against these three powerful enemies, when we consider our extreme weakness, and when we consider the sad fact that the greater part of mankind do not overcome even one of their enemies, we see clearly how terribly true are the words of Our Lord: "Wide is the gate and broad is the way that leadeth to destruction, and many there are who go in thereat. How narrow is the gate and straight is the way that leadeth to life, and few there are that find it." (*Matt.* 7:13-14). Ah, who shall be able to find this straight way! Who will be able to conquer these three enemies of our salvation? Whence shall we obtain strength and courage to struggle bravely against them until death? Truly, we must exclaim with King Josaphat: "As for us, we have not strength enough to be able to resist this multitude, which cometh violently upon us. But as we know not what to do, we can only turn our eyes to thee, our God." (*2 Par.* 20:12). By our own efforts alone we shall not be able to overcome even a single one of our enemies; but, by the strength that God gives to those that ask it, we shall overcome all.

Prayer is that powerful means which God has given us to preserve ourselves in His grace and friendship. Even though it should seem to you that all is lost, that you cannot overcome the temptations of the devil, that you cannot avoid the bad example of the world, that you cannot resist the revolts of corrupt nature, remember that, as St. Paul assures us, God is faithful, and will never suffer you to be tempted beyond your strength, but will make issue, also, with the temptation, that you may be able to bear it. (*1 Cor.* 10:13). But remember, also, that God will give you strength in the hour of temptation, *only on condition that you pray for it; that you pray for it earnestly and perseveringly.* "God," says St. Augustine, "does not command what is impossible; if He commands you to do something, He admonishes you at the same time to do what you can, and to ask Him for His assistance, whenever anything is above your strength, and He promises to assist you to do that which otherwise would naturally be impossible for you to do."

When Publius, the prefect of Rome, tried to persuade St. Felicitas to sacrifice to the gods, she answered: "Do not hope, O Publius, to win me with fair words, or to terrify me with threats; for I have within me the Spirit of God, who will not let me be overcome by Satan, and therefore I am sure I shall be too hard for you, who are the servant of Satan." This is the language that all the just must speak in their hard trials. It is only in prayer that they learn it. St. John Chrysostom also says: "As a city fortified by strong walls cannot be easily taken, so also a soul fortified by prayer cannot be overcome by the devil. The devil is afraid of approaching a soul that prays; he fears the courage and strength that she obtains in prayer; prayer gives more strength to the soul than food does to the body. The more the soul practices prayer, the more will she be nourished and strengthened; and the less she practices prayer, the more keenly will she feel her own natural weakness. As plants cannot remain fresh and green without moisture, air and light, so the soul cannot preserve the grace of God without prayer."

A plant usually prospers only in its native clime. Now the same is true of the soul. The true home of the soul is God; transplant it, and it will not live. Now prayer is the means by which the soul is preserved in this its true home. Prayer keeps the soul united to God, and God to the soul, and thus it lives a perfect life. This is most emphatically expressed by St. John Chrysostom. "Everyone," he says, "who does not pray, and who does not wish to keep in continual communion with God, is dead; he has lost his life, nay, he has even lost his reason; he must be insane, for he does not understand what a great honor it is to pray; and he is not convinced of the important truth that not to pray is to bring death upon his soul, as it is impossible for him to lead a virtuous life without the aid of prayer. For how can he be able to practice virtue without throwing himself unceasingly at the feet of Him from whom alone comes all strength and courage?" (*Lib. de orando Deum*).

St. Augustine also assures that "he who does not know how to pray well, will not know how to live well." (*Homil.*

43). "Nay," says St. Francis of Assisi, "never expect anything good from a soul that is not addicted to prayer." St. Bernard was wont to say: "If I see a man who is not very fond of prayer, I say to myself, that man cannot be virtuous." St. Charles Borromeo says, in one of his pastoral letters that: "Of all means that Jesus Christ has left for our salvation, prayer is the most important." (*Act. Eccl. Med.*, p. 1005). "Indeed," says St. Alphonsus, "in the ordinary course of Providence, our meditations, resolutions, and promises will all be fruitless without prayer, because we will be unfaithful to the Divine inspiration, if we do not pray; in order to be able to overcome temptations, to practice virtue, to keep the commandments of God, we need, besides Divine light, meditations and good resolutions, the *actual assistance* of God. Now this Divine assistance is given to those only who pray for it, and who pray for it unceasingly." (Preface to his book on prayer).

St. Thomas Aquinas asserts that "Adam committed sin because he neglected to pray when he was tempted." St. Gelasius says the same of the fallen angels: "In vain," says he, "did they receive the grace of God; they could not persevere, because they did not pray." (*Epist.* 5, *ad Ep. in P*). St. Macarius tells us (*Hom.* 17) that a certain monk, after having been favored with a wonderful rapture and many great graces, fell, by pride, into several grievous sins. A certain nobleman gave his estate to the poor, and set his slaves at liberty; yet afterwards fell into pride, and many enormous sins. Another, who, in the persecution, had suffered torments with great constancy for the faith, afterward, intoxicated with self-conceit, gave great scandal by his disorders. This saint mentions one who had formerly lived a long time with him in the desert, prayed often with him, and was favored with an extraordinary gift of compunction, and a miraculous power of curing many sick persons, was at last delighted with the glory and applause of men, and drawn into the sin of pride. (*Hom.* 27). St. Alphonsus relates that a certain aged Japanese Christian was condemned to be beheaded on account of his faith. His head was sawed off by slow degrees; he endured this cruel torture for a long time; at last he lost courage, and, ceasing to recommend himself to God, he died an apostate. (*Trials of the Martyrs,* no. 25). Would to God that all might learn, from these sad examples, that our salvation depends on our perseverance in praying to God for aid to resist temptations, and to bear patiently the sufferings and adversities of this life!

Father Segneri relates that a young man named Paccus retired into a wilderness in order to do penance for his sins. After some years of penance he was so violently assaulted by temptations that he thought it impossible to resist them any longer. As he was often overcome by them, he began to despair of his salvation; he even thought of taking away his life. He said to himself that if he must go to Hell, it were better to go instantly than to live on thus in sin, and thereby only increase his torments. One day he took a poisonous viper in his hand, and in every possible manner urged it to bite him; but the reptile did not hurt him in the least. "O God!" cried Paccus, "there are so many who do not wish to die, and I, who wish so much for death, cannot die." At this moment he heard a voice saying to him: "Poor wretch! Do you suppose you can overcome temptations by your own strength? Pray to God for assistance, and He will help you to overcome them." Encouraged by these words, he began to pray most fervently, and soon after lost all his fear. He ever after led a very edifying life.

But why quote examples of this kind? Almost everyone of us can bear witness to the truth that to neglect prayer is to fall into sin, and lose the grace of God. Let everyone who has committed sin ask himself whether he prayed in the moment of temptation, and he will remember that he did not. Every sin, then, which we have committed, is a certain proof of the truth that the grace of God cannot be preserved without continual prayer. Even all the victories which the just have gained over their spiritual enemies will, on the Day of Judgment, be so many evident proofs of this truth. "Christians, then," says Cornelius à Lapide, "cannot make a better use of their leisure time than to spend it in prayer." The saints knew well that prayer was the powerful means to escape the snares of the devil, and therefore they loved and practiced nothing so much as this holy exercise.

King David often prayed to the Lord: "Lord, look upon me and have mercy on me; for I am alone and poor." (*Ps.* 24:16). "I cried with all my whole heart: hear me, O Lord; let thy hand be with me to save me." (*Ps.* 118, 145, 173). He assures us that he prayed without ceasing. "My eyes," said he, "are ever towards the Lord; for he shall pluck my feet out of the snare." (*Ps.* 24:15). "Daniel," says St. John Chrysostom, "preferred to die rather than to give up prayer." St. Philip Neri, being one day commanded to pray a little less than usual, said to one of his fathers: "I begin to feel like a brute." Blessed Leonard of Port-Maurice used to say, a Christian should not let a moment pass by without saying: "My Jesus have mercy on me!" It was by prayer that the saints were enabled to overcome all their temptations, and to suffer patiently all their crosses and persecutions until death; the more they suffered the more they prayed, and the Lord came to their assistance. Thus they gained the crown of eternal life. "He shall cry to me," says the Lord, "and I will hear him; I am with him in tribulation, I will deliver him, and will glorify him." (*Ps.* 90:15). After St. Theodore had been cruelly tortured in many different ways, he was at last commanded by the tyrant to stand on red-hot tiles. Finding this kind of torture almost too great to endure, he prayed to the Lord to alleviate his sufferings, and the Lord granted him courage and fortitude to endure these torments until death. (*Triumphs of the Martyrs,* by St. Alphonsus). St. Perpetua was a lady of noble family, brought up in the greatest luxury, and married to a man of high rank. She had everything to make her cling to this world, for she had not only her husband, but also a father, a mother, and two brothers, of whom she was very fond, and a little baby whom she was nursing. She was only twenty-two years of age, and was of an affectionate and timid disposition, so that she did not seem naturally well-fitted to endure martyrdom with courage, or to bear the separation from her little baby and her aged parents, whom she loved so much.

Although Perpetua loved Jesus, yet she could not help trembling at the thought of the tortures which she would have to suffer. When she was first thrown into prison, she was very much frightened at the darkness of the dungeon; she was half suffocated with the heat and bad air, and she was shocked at the rudeness of the soldiers, who pushed her and the other prisoners about, for she had always lived in a splendid palace, surrounded with every luxury, and had been accustomed from her childhood to be treated with respect. If, then, she shrank from these little trials, what should she do when she was put to the torture, or when she had to face wild beasts in the amphitheater? She was conscious of her own weakness, and at first trembled, but she knew that the heroic virtue of the martyrs did not depend on natural courage and strength; she knew that if she prayed to Jesus, He would give her strength to bear everything, so that the grace of God would shine out most brightly in the midst of her natural weakness.

A few days after she was put to prison she was baptized; and as she came out of the water, the Holy Ghost inspired her *to ask for patience* in all the bodily sufferings which she might be called to endure; so she began to pray very fervently, and from this time she became so calm and so joyful, that in spite of all her own sufferings she was able to cheer and comfort her fellow sufferers.

Thus it is only by prayer that we obtain courage, protection, and fortitude in sufferings and adversities. This we learn especially from the angel who descended with the three children into the fiery furnace. "The angel of the Lord went down with Azarius and his companions into the furnace." (*Dan.* 3:49). "The angel of the Lord had descended into the flames before them, otherwise they would have been immediately consumed; but they did not see him until they prayed to God. After having prayed, they saw how the angel of the Lord drove the flame of the fire out of the furnace, and made the midst of the furnace like the blowing of a wind bringing dew. (*Dan.* 3:49-50). Thus the angel of the Lord," says Cornelius à Lapide, "gives to understand that in persecutions and tribulations prayer is the only means of salvation. Those who pray are always victorious; those who neglect to pray give way to temptations, and are lost."

"I have known many," says St. Cyprian, "and have shed tears over them, who seemed to possess great courage and fortitude of soul, and yet, when on the point of receiving the crown of life everlasting, they fell away and became apostates. Now what was the cause of this? They turned away their eyes from Him who alone is able to give strength to the weak. They had given up prayer, and commenced to look for aid and protection from man; they considered their own natural weakness; they looked at the red-hot gridirons, and at all the other frightful instruments of torture; they compared the acuteness of the pain with their own strength; but as soon as one thinks within himself I can suffer this, but not that, his martyrdom will never be crowned with a glorious end. It was thus that they lost the victory. He only who abandons himself entirely to the Divine will, and who looks for help from God alone, will remain firm and immovable, and persevere to the end. But this can be expected only from him who is gifted with a lively faith, and who does not tremble, or consider how great is the tyrant's cruelty, or how weak is human nature, but who considers only the power of Our Lord Jesus Christ, who fights and conquers in His members. No one should lose courage when he has to endure some great bodily or spiritual affliction. Let him trust in the Lord, whose battles he fights. He will not permit anyone 'to be tempted beyond his strength, but will grant a happy issue to all his sufferings.'"

"We all," says St. Alphonsus, "ought to be firmly convinced that we are, as it were, continually hanging over a frightful abyss of sin, and that we are kept from falling only by a slender thread, which is the grace of Almighty God. If this thread breaks, we instantly fall into the deep, unfathomless abyss of sin, and commit the most atrocious crimes." The governor Paschasius commanded the holy virgin Lucy to be exposed to prostitution in a brothel house; but God rendered her immovable, so that the guards were not able to carry her thither. He also made her an over-match for the cruelty of the persecutors in overcoming fire and other torments. It is only the Lord who can make you immovable in all your good resolutions, it is only His grace that can prevent you from being carried by temptation into the abyss of Hell.

"Unless the Lord had been my helper," says David, "my soul had almost dwelt in hell." (*Ps.* 93:17). And, "Unless the Lord keep the city, he watcheth in vain that keepeth it." (*Ps.* 126:1). Unless the Lord preserves the soul from sin, all her endeavors to avoid it will be fruitless. "Lord," exclaimed St. Philip Neri, "keep Thy hand over me this day, otherwise Thou will be betrayed by Philip."

Now what a St. Augustine, a St. Cyprian, a St. John Chrysostom, a St. Alphonsus, and so many other saints have said of prayer as being a most necessary means to preserve the grace of God until death, is confirmed by many of the clearest passages of Holy Writ. How did it happen that those two elders went so far in their wickedness as to tempt the chaste Susanna? It was, as the prophet Daniel says, because "They perverted their own mind and turned away their eyes, that they might not look unto heaven, nor remember just judgments." (*Dan.* 13:9). "The impious," says David, "in general are corrupt, and they become abominable in their ways. . . . They are all gone aside; they are become unprofitable together; there is none that does good—no, not one. . . . Destruction and unhappiness are in their ways." What is the cause of all this? "It is," continues David, "because they have not called upon the Lord."

"For him, then," says St. Isidore,"who is assailed with temptation, there is no other remedy left than prayer, to which he must have recourse as often as he is tempted. Frequent recourse to prayer subdues all temptations to sin." (*Lib.* III *De summo bono,* chap. 8). "Which of the just," asks St. John Chrysostom, "did ever fight valiantly without prayer? Which of them ever conquered without prayer?" (*Sermo de Mose*). Neither any of the Apostles, nor any of the martyrs, nor any of the confessors, nor any of the holy virgins and widows, nor any of the just in Heaven or on earth.

Father Hunolt, S.J., says that to hope to remain free from sin, and persevere in virtue, and be saved without prayer, is to tempt God—is to require of Him a miracle; it is just as absurd as to imagine that you can see without eyes, hear without ears, and walk without feet. Of this, my dear reader, you also should be firmly convinced. Let us, then, as St. Bernard admonishes us, always have recourse to prayer as to the surest weapon of defense. Let prayer be your first act in the morning. Have recourse to prayer whenever you feel tempted to lukewarmness, to impatience, to impurity, or to any other sin. Arm yourself with prayer when you have to mingle with the wicked world, or when you have to fight against your corrupt nature. Let prayer never leave your heart; let it never desert your lips; let prayer be your constant companion on all your journeys; let prayer close your eyes at night; let prayer be your exercise of predilection. Every other loss may be repaired, but the loss of prayer never. If, on account of a delicate constitution, you cannot fast, you may give alms; if you have no opportunity to confess your sins, you may obtain the forgiveness of them by an act of perfect contrition; nay, even Baptism itself may sometimes be supplied by an earnest desire for this sacrament, accompanied by an ardent love for God. But as for him who neglects to practice prayer, there is no other means of salvation left. Give up every other occupation rather than neglect prayer. Persevere in prayer, as all the saints have done; follow the example of our Divine Saviour, who prayed even to the very last moment of His life, and leave this world with prayer upon your lips. Thus prayer will conduct you to Heaven, there to reign eternally with Our Lord Jesus Christ, and all the just, in everlasting joy and glory.

Chapter 5

ON THE NECESSITY OF
PRAYER FOR SEMINARIANS

"Lord, teach us to pray, as John also taught his disciples."—*Luke* 11:1.

One of the most important duties of a pastor is to teach the people the necessity and efficacy of prayer, and how they are to pray, and for what they are to pray. Hence it is said, in the Catechism of the Council of Trent, that "Amongst the duties of the pastoral office, it is one of the highest importance to the spiritual interest of the faithful to instruct them in Christian prayer, the nature and efficacy of which must be unknown to many, if not enforced by the pious and faithful exhortations of the pastor. To this, therefore, should the care of the pastor be directed in a special manner, that the faithful may understand how, and for what, they are to pray."

Oh, how unspeakable is the pleasure given to Jesus Christ by a pastor, who often in public, as well as in private, fulfills this duty! Would to God that all pastors would adopt the sentiments of St. Alphonsus, and could say with him: "I wish I had nothing else to do than to speak and to write on this great means of prayer; for, on the one hand, I see that the Holy Scriptures, including both the Old and New Testament, exhort us to pray, to ask and cry aloud if we wish for Divine grace; and on the other hand, I must openly confess that I cannot help complaining of preachers, confessors, and spiritual writers, because I see that none of them speak as much as they ought of the great means of prayer. And in the many courses of Lenten sermons which have been published, where shall we find a discourse on prayer? Scarcely do we find a few passing words concerning this important means of grace. Hence I have written at length on this subject in so many of my little works, and whenever I preach, I always repeat these words: 'Pray, pray, if you wish to be saved, and to become saints.' It is true that, to become saints, we must have all virtues, mortification, humility, obedience, and principally holy charity; and to acquire these virtues other means besides prayer are necessary, such as meditation, Holy Communion, and good resolutions; but, unless we pray, all our Communions, meditations, and resolutions will not suffice to make us practice either mortification, humility, or obedience. We will neither love God nor resist temptations; in a word, we will do no good. Hence St. Paul, after having enumerated many of the virtues necessary for a Christian, tells us to be 'instant in prayer' (*Rom.* 12:12), thereby giving us to understand, as St. Thomas remarks, 'that to acquire all necessary virtues we must always pray, because without prayer we would be deprived of the assistance of God, without which it is impossible to practice virtue.'" (*Spouse of Christ on Prayer*, No. 13).

These sentiments of St. Alphonsus were common to all the saints. Should you ever hear anyone oppose them, rest assured that he cannot say in truth, with St. Paul: "I think that I also have the spirit of God" (*1 Cor.* 7:40); nor should you believe that he is "of the seed of those men by whom salvation was brought to Israel." (*1 Mach.* 5:62).

Let us, in imitation of the saints, never grow weary of repeating this sacred truth in public and in private. What St. Augustine says is but too true. "The understanding flies on," he says, "but resolution and action follow slowly, or not at all." Our will is weaker to do what is right, than our understanding is to comprehend it. The people, then, must often be told the same thing. St. Paul himself assures us of this: "To write the same things to you," he says, "to me is not wearisome, but to you is necessary." (*Phil.* 3:1). The Apostle was not in want of matter to write, for he who had been wrapt to the third heaven was certainly able to say many new and sublime things, but he deemed it profitable, and even necessary, for the faithful to write to them the same thing again and again.

It was the opinion of St. Francis de Sales that "a preacher should not take the least notice of those fastidious minds who are displeased when a preacher repeats a thing, and goes over the same ground again. What! Is it not necessary, in working iron, to heat it over and over again, and in painting, to touch and retouch the canvas repeatedly? How much more necessary, then, is it not to repeat the same thing again and again, in order to imprint eternal truths on hardened intellects, and on hearts confirmed in evil?" Now, what can be more necessary and more profitable than often to imprint on souls the necessity of prayer?

How, then, does it happen that so many pastors neglect to comply with this most essential duty? It is principally because they themselves have never learned how necessary prayer is, and how efficacious, if performed well.

No one can speak of what he knows not, nor give what he does not possess. To be able to discharge this pastoral duty properly, a priest must have learned, whilst as yet a student, to lead a holy life, and to practice faithfully meditation and prayer. For this reason I have thought it necessary to insert a chapter on the great obligation which ecclesiastical students have to sanctify themselves in the time of their studies by the practice of solid virtue, and especially by prayer and meditation. And, first of all, I must remark that I am far from believing that all who study for the priesthood are called to this sublime office. Alas! There are but too many who study from low and worldly motives, and seek in the ecclesiastical state nothing but temporal advantages. To this kind of students I have but a few words to say.

My dear young friends, I conjure you, by the love of Our Lord Jesus Christ, consider well that, in order to save your souls, you must embrace that state of life to which God has called you; for in that state alone you occupy the place for which God has destined you from all eternity, and in that state He will give you all the graces necessary to fulfill all your duties. If you live out of the state to which you are called, it will be very difficult, nay, almost impossible, for you to work out your salvation. This is true of everyone who lives in a state of life to which God has not called him, but it is especially true of all those who have chosen the ecclesiastical state without being called thereto by God. This is evident; for, in the first place, it is grievous presumption in anyone to dare enter into the Holy of Holies without having a clearly Divine vocation. Moreover, everyone who enters this holy state without being called thereto by God, will be deprived of the proper means and graces to comply with the duties of this holy state; and even though he should be able to comply with these duties, yet, having strayed away from the right road, he will find every other very steep and difficult, and he will be like a dislocated member, which, indeed, may still perform some services, but not without great difficulty and many defects.

Anyone who receives Holy Orders without having the signs of a true vocation from God becomes guilty of mortal sin. This is the teaching of St. Alphonsus, and of many other learned theologians, especially of St. Augustine, who says, when speaking of the punishment of Core, Dathan and Abiron, who wished to exercise the functions of High Priest without being called thereto, "they were condemned, in order than everyone might be deterred from taking upon himself the office of High Priest without being called thereto by God. This terrible fate will befall all those deacons, priests, and bishops who enter or intrude themselves into the ecclesiastical state from mere worldly motives, and without being called thereto by God." (Sermon 98). St. Ephrem considers as reprobates all those who dare become priests without a Divine vocation. "I am astounded," says he, "at the madness of those who are so presumptuous as to perform the functions of the priesthood without having grace for it from Jesus Christ. Unhappy wretches! They do not consider that by doing so they are preparing for themselves everlasting torments." (*De Sacerdot*). I would therefore earnestly urge all those young men who are studying for the priesthood, without having an evident vocation, to give up the idea as soon as possible. The sooner they do this the better it is for themselves, and for thousands of others.

I will now turn to those students whom Jesus Christ has really called, and to whom the words of the Gospel may be applied: "You have not chosen me, but I have chosen you." (*John* 15:16). My dear young friends, consider well the high dignity to which you are called. The priesthood is the highest dignity on earth. Innocent III says, "The priest is placed between God and man; he is less than God, but more than man." This dignity supposes, besides the Divine vocation, positive holiness of life; that is to say, whosoever intends to embrace the ecclesiastical state must not only be free from mortal sin, but he must also be enriched with every virtue. The Church, during eleven centuries, excluded from this holy state everyone who had committed even one mortal sin after Baptism; and if anyone, after having received Holy Orders, fell into a mortal sin, he was deposed forever from his sacred office, for the simple reason that he who is not holy should not touch what is holy.

This severe discipline of the Church, it is true, has been greatly mitigated; but it has been always required that he who had in his past life become guilty of grievous sins, and desired to receive Holy Orders, should first lead a pure life for some time previous to his ordination. It would certainly be a mortal sin to receive any of the Holy Orders while still addicted to a sinful habit. "If I consider your vocation," says St. Bernard, "I am seized with horror, especially if I see that no true penance has preceded your ordination."

Many of the saints would never consent to receive Holy Orders. St. Francis of Assisi once beheld, in a vision, a crystal vase filled with most limpid water. God revealed to him that the soul of a priest must be as pure as this crystal vase. This vision made such a deep impression upon him that he could never afterwards be prevailed upon to accept the dignity of the priesthood.

The Abbot Theodore had received the Order of Deacon. One day he beheld a fiery column, and heard, at the same time, a voice, saying: "If thy heart be as fiery as this column, thou mayest exercise the functions of thy sacred Order." He could never afterwards consent to exercise these sacred functions. Everyone, even the most perverse, feels naturally that the candidate for the priesthood should be holy; the least fault in him is considered unpardonable.

"I have appointed you," says Our Lord Jesus Christ,

"that you should go and should bring forth fruit, and that your fruit should remain." (*John* 15:16). Now a student will not bring forth this fruit, that is to say, holiness of life, unless he seriously endeavors, in the course of his studies, to sanctify himself. Let him not imagine that sanctity will be infused into his soul by the sacrament of Holy Orders; let him rest assured that, if he is not a virtuous student, he will never be a virtuous priest. A light-minded student will be a light-minded priest; a proud, immortified and sensual student will make a proud, immortified and sensual priest.

It is true, you must study to acquire the necessary science, without which you would be unfit for the sacred ministry. But, my dear young friends, it is not learning, but purity of life, that will qualify you for the priesthood. A certain author says, "Those who know that their hearts are enslaved by sinful habits, and still dare to receive Holy Orders, should rather be led to a place of execution than to the Church of God." It is not enough for the candidate for the priesthood to be free from sin; he must, moreover, have led a pious life, and have acquired a certain facility in the practice of virtue. Should a candidate for any of the Holy Orders be addicted to some sinful habit at the time of his ordination, he is, according to the opinion of theologians, unworthy to receive even the sacrament of Penance, even though he should otherwise be properly disposed. For in order to receive the sacrament of Penance worthily at such a time, he must also be properly disposed to receive that of Holy Orders. A confessor who knowingly and willfully would absolve such a candidate, would thereby become guilty of mortal sin; and should he give him a good testimonial, so that the young candidate would on that account be promoted to Holy Orders, such a confessor would become answerable for all the sins committed by this unworthy priest during the whole course of his ministry.

Whoever, then, wishes to receive Holy Orders worthily, must necessarily lead a virtuous life. According to St. Thomas Aquinas, a priest must be possessed of greater interior holiness than even a religious, on account of the holy and sublime functions of the sacred ministry, and especially because he has to offer up so often the most august Sacrifice of the Mass.

I do not fear so much that students will fail to acquire sufficient knowledge, but I fear very much that they will not acquire sufficient holiness of life before receiving Holy Orders. I have always observed that the greater number of ecclesiastical students make great efforts to acquire sufficient knowledge; but few indeed are those who earnestly strive to lead a holy life. The natural ambition to appear learned before others, and the thought that they will have to preach one day in presence of heretics and unbelievers, induce them to make every exertion to learn how to refute every error, and to defend the truths of our holy religion. They apply themselves so seriously to their studies, that their mind is altogether taken up with them. This is especially the case when they consider the actual state of society, and the infidel and immoral principles that prevail everywhere. It is, indeed, only too true that we live in a most anti-Christian age; principles are disregarded, and iniquity is held in veneration; we see nothing but confusion in religion, in government, in the family circle. Sects spring up and swarm like locusts, destroying not only revealed religion, but rejecting even the law of nature. Fraud, theft, and robbery are practiced, almost as a common trade. The press justifies rebellion, secret societies, and plots for the overthrow of established governments. The civil law, by granting divorce, has broken the family tie. Children are allowed to grow up in ignorance of true religious principles; their fathers being without religion, or given up to the most detestable vices, or their mothers destitute of virtue, and infected in the highest degree with the spirit of vanity, the natural consequence is, that these children are regardless of their parents. The number of apostates is on the increase, at least in the younger generation: Immoral books and tracts circulate freely; daily journals, weekly magazines, the great organs of public opinion, become more unchristian every day; so much so, that no one who has at heart the morality of his fellow men, especially of youth, can, with propriety, recommend them for perusal; and yet how eagerly are they sought for and devoured by every class of men!

Such diseases of the human mind and heart, the student will think, require remedy. To counteract and heal them, he will think, will require great learning and experience, and that consequently a thorough and earnest study of philosophy and theology will be absolutely necessary. But here lies the stumbling block for the greater number of students: They endeavor rather to cultivate the mind than the heart; they are more desirous to fill their memory with the principles of philosophy and other profane sciences, than with the principles of Jesus Christ and His saints; they care more to know their lessons well, than to make a good meditation; they take more pains to appear well-prepared before their professors and schoolmates, than before Jesus Christ in Holy Communion; they make greater efforts to compose a good discourse, than to make a good examination of conscience; they long more ardently to acquire a reputation for learning and great talents, than they do to acquire the virtues of humility and sincere charity; they are more pleased with the praises of the world, than with the good pleasure of Jesus Christ. Clearness in reasoning, and ability in delivering a learned discourse, is, in their opinion, of more importance than the spirit of meekness, condescension, and submission in all their words and actions. They take more pleasure in reading profane, frivolous books, than such as nourish piety and inspire love for solitude and prayer. In a word, they make greater efforts to acquire the wisdom of the world than that of Jesus Christ and His saints. Thus study, instead of uniting them more closely with God, only separates them farther from Him.

I do not by any means wish to blame students for applying themselves to study. What I blame in them, is the manner in which they apply themselves.

Learning can do much good, it is true; but however much it may accomplish, experience teaches us, in the present as in the past, that moral evils never yield to any other force than the grace of God. A learned man may enlighten the minds of his fellow men, and expel their darkness and errors, but unless the grace of God touch their hearts, they will not embrace the truth. "It is neither philosophy," wrote St. Vincent de Paul to one of his priests, "nor theology, nor eloquence alone, that moves the soul." This truth was felt most keenly by St. Bernard whilst at Paris, 1123. He had scarcely arrived in the capital, when he was pressed to deliver a discourse at the Academy of Philosophy and Theology. He yielded to this invitation, and, having to speak before a numerous assembly, he prepared himself with care, and pronounced a learned dissertation on the most sublime questions of philosophy; but when he had finished his discourse, the audience remained cold and unmoved.

Alas, there are but too many who imitate St. Bernard in this point! Like him, they, too, know how to prepare very learned discourses; they use the most eloquent language. They may indeed enlighten the mind, but they do not reach the heart. The only fruits their sermons produce are a few unmeaning flatteries, which serve only to nourish their pride and self-love. "What a magnificent sermon!" the people will say; "What an eloquent speaker! What profound knowledge! What a clear mind! What a fascinating preacher! What a pleasure it is to listen to such a man! I never had such a treat in my life!" Would to God these preachers would imitate St. Bernard in his preparation for his second discourse! How different would be the fruit of their labors!

When this saint had finished his first discourse, and saw how his audience remained cold and unmoved, he withdrew in sadness and confusion; he shut himself up in an oratory, where he sighed and wept abundantly before God. On the morrow, St. Bernard presented himself again in the same school; "But this time," says the author of the Exordium of Citeaux, "the Holy Ghost spoke by his mouth, and guided his lips; and the admirable discourse which he pronounced made such an impression, that many ecclesiastics, being deeply moved by it placed themselves under his direction, and followed him to Clairvaux, there to serve God under his guidance." It is related in the life of this saint, that mothers used to keep their children, wives their husbands, and friends their friends, from listening to him, because the Holy Ghost gave so great a power to his words that no one could resist them; everyone felt inspired to follow him, or at least to lead a better life.

After John Tauler had shone in the pulpit for many years, and won applause in Cologne and all Germany, he suddenly retreated to his cell, leaving the people astonished at his disappearance. The fact was, an unknown man accosted him after one of his discourses, and asked permission to speak his mind regarding him. Tauler having given this permission, the unknown replied: "There lives in your heart a secret pride; you rely on your great learning, and your title of Doctor. In the study of letters you do not seek God or His glory with a pure intention, you seek only yourself in the passing applause of creatures. Therefore the wine of heavenly doctrine and the

Divine Word, though pure and excellent in themselves, lose their strength when passing through your heart, and drop without savor or grace into the breast that loves God." (*Tauler's Life,* by Darius, B. D.). Tauler was magnanimous enough to listen to these words, and assuredly no one would have ventured so to address him, had he not deserved it. He kept silence. The vanity of his present life was apparent to him. Withdrawn from all commerce with the world, he abstained for two years from preaching or hearing confessions, night and day an assiduous attendant at every conventual exercise, and passing the remainder of his time in his cell, deploring his sins and studying Jesus Christ. After two years, Cologne learned that Doctor Tauler was to preach once more. The entire city repaired to the church, curious to penetrate the mystery of a retirement which had been variously explained; but when he ascended the pulpit, after vain struggles to speak, tears were the only thing he could bring from his heart; he was now not merely an orator, he was a saint.

Let us hear what the saints say in reference to mere worldly wisdom. "You must consider," says St. Vincent de Paul, "that learning without humility has always done great harm to the Church; that pride has always brought the greater part of learned men, like the rebellious angels, to everlasting perdition. God does not need learned men to carry out His wise designs. Generally speaking, He makes use of the simple to convert men, and procure the welfare of His Church. This we see in the case of the Apostles, and, in recent times, of St. Catherine of Siena, and of St. Teresa"; and I may add, in our own days, of the Curé of Ars, in France. St. Ignatius Loyola says: "It is of greater importance for students to advance in virtue than in science; if they cannot do both at the same time, virtue must have the preference—*minus scientiae, plus virtutis.*" (*Life,* by C. Genelli).

St. Francis of Assisi said to those who wished to enter his Order and had already completed their course of studies, and wished to apply themselves solely to the study of Holy Scripture: "I am well pleased with such, provided, according to the example of Jesus Christ, who seems to have devoted more time to prayer than to anything else, they do not neglect the exercise of prayer, and endeavor rather to practice what they have learned than to learn new things, which they will probably never practice. The truths of the Gospel are better understood by those who practice them, than by those who know them but neglect to put them into practice. A man possesses knowledge and eloquence only in proportion as he practices what he knows and teaches. Many think they will find happiness in acquiring great learning; but truly happy is he only who knows Jesus Christ, and Him crucified."

Studies undertaken with a view to gain the applause of men, were always an abomination in the eyes of this great saint. He used to say of these vain men, that on the day of retribution they would find their hands empty; that they should rather strive now to acquire solid virtue, and advance in the grace of God; for the time will come when books and worldly learning will be rejected as useless. You should, therefore, earnestly endeavor, beloved brethren, to acquire the virtues of humility, simplicity, prayer, and the love of holy poverty. This is the only sure way of edifying your neighbor, and of procuring his salvation; for you are called to imitate Jesus Christ, who did not point out to us any other road to Heaven. Many abandon these virtues, under the specious pretext of edifying their neighbor by their learning; but they are greatly deceived if they think that by great learning alone they can fill the hearts of their fellow men with light, devotion, and love for God. Learning only puffs up such vain men, and extinguishes the love of God in their hearts. Hence it usually comes to pass that after having wasted their time in useless studies, instead of striving to live up to the spirit of their vocation they will find themselves incapable of returning to their original fervor.

Father John de Starchia, Provincial of the Friar Minors in Lombardy, having been upbraided in vain by St. Francis of Assisi for introducing an excessive application of study and making regulations more promotive of science than of piety, was publicly cursed by this saint, and deposed at the ensuing chapter. The saint, on being entreated to withdraw this curse and give his blessing to brother John, who was a learned nobleman, answered: "I cannot bless him whom the Lord has cursed." A dreadful reply, which was soon after verified. This unfortunate man died exclaiming: "I am damned and cursed for all eternity." Some frightful circumstances, which took place after his death, confirmed this fearful prediction.

St. Francis was by no means averse to the acquisition of learning; on the contrary, he exhorted those of his brethren whose duty it was to teach, to apply themselves diligently to study. But he was always opposed to that vain and worldly wisdom which is always without devotion, and which preaches itself instead of Jesus Christ crucified. He often repeated these words of Holy Writ: "Many will say to me in that day: Lord, Lord, have not we prophesied in thy name, and cast out devils in thy name, and done many miracles in thy name? And then will I profess unto them, I never knew you: depart from me, you that work iniquity." (*Matt.* 7:22-23).

St. Francis knew full well that man is naturally more inclined to learn the truth than to practice it, and that virtue, which purifies the soul, is far more precious and far more necessary than learning, which enlightens the mind.

St. Alphonsus speaks in the same manner: "The Apostle St. Paul," says he, "wrote of the world's wisdom:

'Knowledge puffeth up, but charity edifieth. If any man think he knoweth anything, he hath not yet known as he ought to know.' (*1 Cor.* 8:1). Knowledge, united to the love of God, is most useful to us and to our neighbor; but if charity does not accompany it, it does us much harm, by making us proud, and leading us to despise others; 'for the Lord is merciful to the humble, but He resisteth the proud.' Happy is the man to whom God has given the science of the saints. This science He gave to the righteous Abel, upon whom, as Holy Scripture assures us, 'He bestowed the knowledge of the holy things.' (*Wis.* 10:10).

"The Holy Spirit speaks of the science of the saints as being the greatest of all gifts. How many do we not see who are puffed up on account of their knowledge of mathematics, philology, archaeology, and philosophy. But what does religion gain by their knowledge? What gain do so many learned men derive from all their knowledge, if they have not yet even learned how to love God and to practice virtue? The Lord refuses His light to those wise ones of the world who labor only to gain applause of men, and He grants His gifts only to the pure and simple of heart. 'I confess to thee, O Father, Lord of heaven and earth,' says our Divine Saviour, 'because thou hast hid these things from the wise and prudent, and hast revealed them to the little ones.' (*Matt.* 11:25). 'Happy is he,' says St. Augustine, 'who knows God, His greatness and His goodness, though he be ignorant of all besides; for he who knows God cannot help loving Him. Now he who loves is wiser than all the learned of the earth who know not to love. The ignorant arise, and win Heaven.' How many ignorant people, how many poor peasants, sanctify themselves daily, and gain eternal life! St. Paul writes to the Corinthians: 'I judged not myself to know anything among you, but Jesus Christ, and Him crucified.' Happy are we if we acquire the knowledge of Jesus Christ, of the love He has shown us on the Cross.

"We must study, it is true, because we are laborers; but we ought to be fully convinced that the one thing needful which Jesus Christ requires, above everything else, is that we should strive to be saved as saints. We must study, but the sole object of our study ought to be to please God; otherwise our studies will cause us to remain longer in Purgatory, nay, may even cause some of us—which may God forbid—to be cast in the everlasting flames of Hell. Let your aim, then, always be the glory of God and the salvation of souls; and when an opportunity of appearing ignorant occurs, do not recoil from it."

St. Alphonsus wrote to his students, after the departure of a certain professor, who had introduced among them an excessive application to study: "I am not sorry when I see you retrench your studies, and give more time to prayer. We have been called to succor poor destitute souls; we have therefore more need of sanctity than of science. If we are not holy, we are exposed to the danger of falling into a thousand imperfections. I repeat it once more, if you retrench somewhat from your studies in order to apply yourselves more diligently to prayer, far from being sorry, I shall, on the contrary, feel greatly consoled." (*Life*, by Father Tanoja, Vol. V, p. 34).

An ecclesiastical student, then, must bear in mind that knowledge without the love of God is nothing but "a sounding brass and tinkling cymbal." "If I speak with the tongues of men and of angels, and have not charity, I am become a sounding brass, or a tinkling cymbal." (*1 Cor.* 13:1). The venerable Father Alvarez, S.J., took all possible care that study should not weaken the piety of the students under his charge. To succeed in this, he adopted the following means:

Above all, he inculcated on the students such striking truths as these: "Virtue and knowledge are the two trees planted by God in Paradise; they are the two great luminaries created by God to give light to the world; they are the two Testaments, the Old and New; they are the two sisters, Martha and Mary, living under one roof in great union and harmony, and mutually supporting each other. Holiness gives to knowledge, authority and solidity. The Apostle St. Paul writes to his disciple Timothy: 'Take heed to thyself and to doctrine; for in doing this thou shalt save both thyself and them that hear thee.'" (*1 Tim.* 4:16). Commenting on this advice of St. Paul, Father Alvarez says: "We acquire knowledge in proportion as we endeavor to acquire virtue. Who is there that does not know that knowledge is a gift of God, and that God bestows this gift upon us in proportion as we purify our hearts? An ecclesiastical student, then, should make greater efforts to avoid sin, and correct his faults, than to study learned authors, and peruse many books."

This zealous director of souls was also very careful to inspire the students with love of mortification, as a powerful means to make them advance both in perfection and science. "But some will ask," says he, "how can mortification be a means of advancing in science? All I answer is, try it, and you will experience that there is nothing which removes all difficulties more surely than mortification. By the practice of mortification you will easily overcome the inordinate desire to study at the time when you are engaged in prayer. Mortification will teach you to overcome your pride, when you feel offended at some question of the professor, or at the objections of your fellow students. Mortification will induce you to apply yourselves only to such branches of science as are assigned to you, and to learn only what is useful, and not what nourishes curiosity. If you love mortification, you will prefer the views of your professor to your own, *i.e.,* provided they are not evidently against faith and morals. This was the advice of St. Augustine, who says: 'That student knows much, who knows how to profit by the teachings of his professor.' As the professor is gifted with knowledge, so must the student be endowed with docility. It belongs to the professor to judge what is fit for him, and to point out the studies best calculated to cultivate his mind.

"The spirit of mortification will prevent you from boasting before others of your knowledge; it will teach you to study diligently, and to overcome all dislike and weariness in your studies; it will enable you to study without too great haste. There is no greater obstacle to the acquisition of solid science, than over-haste in studying; this over-great haste will cause you to study everything superficially. As discretion is a virtue, so is too great eagerness a fault, which must be avoided. *'Sapere, et sapere ad sobrietatem!'* The spirit of mortification will enable you to overcome that foolish shame which you may feel in asking for an explanation when you are in doubt; it will also teach you to be diligent in taking notes of whatever you may find of utility in the books which you read, or in the observations of your professor. *'Multa scribendo didici,'* says St. Augustine. It will keep you from reading books which are forbidden by your professor, and which would only take away your mind from your studies.

"'To study well,' says St. Bernard, 'we must know the true end for which we study. We must not study in order to nourish our vainglory or to gratify our curiosity; but we must study in order to sanctify ourselves, and edify our neighbor. There are some who wish to know merely for the sake of knowing; this is detestable curiosity. Others wish to know in order to become known; this is execrable vanity. Others, again, study in order to sell their science; this is filthy lucre. But there are others who study in order to be able to edify their fellow men; this is charity. Others, again, study in order to edify themselves; this is wisdom.

The two latter classes of students only, do not abuse knowledge; for they study only to do good.'" (*Serm.* 26, in *Cant.*).

Father Alvarez also made every effort to inspire the students with a great love for prayer, as he knew by his own experience that it is a most efficacious means of making rapid progress in science and in virtue. His modesty would not allow him to speak of himself; hence he used to cite to his students the example of the Abbot Theodore, who, as Cassian assures us, had acquired great learning more by assiduous application to prayer, and by purifying his heart, than by studying many books. One day this holy abbot, wishing to find out the meaning of a certain passage of Holy Scripture, began to study diligently, but all his efforts were in vain. At last he commenced to pray for light, and instantly he understood its meaning. (*Life of Father Alvarez*).

St. Thomas Aquinas confessed publicly that he owed his wisdom more to prayer than to his efforts in studying. There are numerous examples of this kind to be found in the lives of the Fathers of the Desert. In our own times we have, in the Curé of Ars, a most striking proof of the wonderful power of prayer in enlightening the understanding. How could this man, who, on account of his want of talent, had so much difficulty in being admitted into the seminary, and who had, since his promotion to the priesthood, spent all his time in prayer and in the labors of the confessional, how, I ask, could he have acquired the power to teach like one of the Fathers of the Church? Whence did he derive his astonishing knowledge of God, of nature, and of the human soul? How came it that his thoughts and expressions so often coincided with those of the greatest minds in the Church; of a St. Augustine, a St. Bernard, a St. Thomas Aquinas? The Spirit of God was pleased to engrave on the heart of this holy priest all that he should know and teach to others. His lively faith was the great fountainhead whence he drew all his wisdom. His "book" was the death and the Cross of Our Lord Jesus Christ. To him all other science was vain and useless. He sought wisdom not amid the dusty tomes of libraries, not in the schools of philosophy, but in prayer, kneeling at his Master's feet, and covering these Divine feet with his kisses and tears. It was in the presence of his Divine Lord, hidden in the Sacrament of His love, that he learned all his wisdom. Prayer, then, is certainly a most powerful means to acquire true and solid wisdom. "If anyone wants wisdom," says St. James, "let him ask it of God, who giveth to all men abundantly, and it shall be given to him." (*James* 1:5).

In order to be able to draw souls to God, we ourselves must first be united to God. Now it is especially in prayer that God unites the soul to Himself. We see in the lives of St. Dominic, St. Francis Xavier, St. Francis Regis, St. Alphonsus, St. Leonard of Port-Maurice, that these holy men, after having labored during the day for the salvation of souls, were wont, after the example of Our Lord Jesus Christ, to spend the greater part of the night in prayer. St. Francis de Sales declared that "The masses and prayers which he offered up for the inhabitants of Chablais contributed more toward their conversion than all his learning. The Apostles," said he, "never preached the Word of God without having first offered up most fervent prayers to Heaven. He is greatly mistaken who expects to convert infidels, heretics, or other great sinners, by any other means than those which Jesus Christ and His Apostles employed; it is God alone who, by His grace, changes the hearts of men, and for this grace we can never pray too fervently."

"The labors of a priest who is not given to prayer," says St. Vincent de Paul, "will produce little or no good;

whilst, on the contrary, a priest who is given to prayer can easily move the hearts of his hearers, and convert even the most hardened sinners. Yes, give me a man of prayer, and all his efforts will be crowned with success. He will be able to say with St. Paul: 'I can do all things in Him who strengtheneth me!' Prayer is the grand fountainhead from which he can derive true eloquence to inspire the hearts of the people with horror of sin and love of virtue." Indeed, the priest who diligently practices prayer may say with Our Lord Jesus Christ: "I speak that which I have seen with my Father" (*John* 8:38); he can also say with St. John: "That which was from the beginning, which we have heard, which we have seen with our eyes, which we have looked upon . . . we declare unto you, that you also may have fellowship with us, and our fellowship may be with the Father, and with his Son Jesus Christ." (*1 John* 1-3).

The Curé of Ars is a most admirable example of this truth. When the people heard this saintly priest, who made no pretensions to learning, speak of Heaven, of the Sacred Humanity of Our Lord, of His sorrowful Passion, His real presence in the Most Holy Sacrament of the Altar, when they heard him discourse of the Blessed Virgin Mary, of her mercy and greatness, when they heard him speak of the happiness of the saints, the purity of the angels, the beauty of a pure soul, the dignity of man, of all those subjects which were familiar to him, when the people, I say, heard this saintly priest speak of all these subjects, they generally came away from the discourse quite convinced that the good father had seen the things of which he spoke with such fullness of heart, with such lively emotions, and with such an abundance of tears. Indeed, his words then bore the impress of Divine tenderness; they penetrated the heart with a warmth and unction which was undescribable. There was so extraordinary a majesty, so marvelous a power in his voice, in his gestures, and in his looks, that it was impossible to listen to him without being moved.

Views and sentiments which are imparted to the soul by God produce a far different impression from those which are acquired by study. Doubt gave way, even in the most darkened minds, to the absolute certainty of faith. The words of the Curé of Ars were the most efficacious, because he preached from his inmost heart. His very appearance was a living proof of the truth of what he said. It could be truly said of him, that he was able to convince men even by his silence. When you saw that pale and emaciated face in the pulpit—when you heard that shrill, piercing voice uttering such sublime thoughts, clothed in the most simple and popular language—you naturally fancied yourself in the presence of one of those great characters spoken of in the Bible. You already felt yourself filled with respect and confidence, and disposed not to criticize his words, but to profit by them.

To those to whom it was given to assist at his catechetical instructions, two things were equally remarkable—the preacher and the hearer. They were not the words that the preacher gave forth—it was more than words; it was a soul, a holy soul, all filled with faith and love, that poured itself out before you, of which you felt in your own soul the immediate contact, and the warmth. As for the hearer, he was no longer on the earth; he was transported into those purer regions, from which dogmas and mysteries descend. As the saint spoke, new and clear views opened to the mind—Heaven and earth, the present and the future life, the things of time and eternity, appeared in a light that you have never before perceived.

When a man coming fresh from the world, and bringing with him worldly ideas, feelings and impressions, sat down to listen to his doctrine, it stunned and amazed him; it set the world so utterly at defiance, and all that the world believes, loves and extols. At first he was astonished and thunderstruck, then by degrees he was touched, and surprised into weeping like the rest.

No eloquence has drawn forth more tears, or penetrated deeper into the hearts of men. His words opened a way before them like flames, and the most hardened hearts melted like wax before the fire. They were burning, radiating, triumphant; they did more than charm the mind; they subdued the whole soul, and brought it back to God: not by the long and difficult way of argument, but by the paths of emotion, which lead shortly and directly to the desired end.

He was the oracle that people went to consult, that they might learn to know Jesus Christ. Not only the sinful, but the learned, not only the fervent, but the indifferent, found in it a Divine unction which penetrated them, and made them long to hear it again. The more often you heard him, the more you desired to go and hear him again and again. Nothing more clearly showed that the Curé of Ars was full of the Spirit of God, who alone is greater than our heart. We may draw from His depths without ever exhausting them; and the Divine satiety which He gives only excites a greater appetite.

He spoke without any other preparation than his continual union with God. He passed, without interval or delay, from the confessional to the pulpit; and yet he showed an imperturbable confidence, which sprang from complete and absolute forgetfulness of himself. Besides, no one was tempted to criticize him. People generally criticize those who are not indifferent to their opinion of them. Those who heard the Curé of Ars had something else to do—they had to pass judgment on themselves.

This real power of his word supplied in him the want of talent and rhetoric. It gave a singular majesty and an irresistible authority to the most simple things that issued from those venerable lips. He loosened his words like arrows from the bow, and his whole soul seemed to fly with them.

In these effusions, the pathetic, the profound, the sublime, was often side by side with the simple and the ordinary. They had all the freedom and irregularity, but also all the originality and power, of an improvization. Those who have sometimes tried to write down what they had just heard, found it impossible to recall the things which had most moved them, and to put them into form. What is most divine in the heart of man cannot be expressed in writing.

"Experience," says St. Thomas of Villanova, "shows us every day that a priest of moderate learning, but full of the love of Jesus Christ, converts more souls than many learned orators, whose eloquent discourses are praised by everyone." St. Jerome used to say: "One single priest inflamed with Divine love, is able to convert a whole nation." "One word," says St. Alphonsus, "uttered by a priest inflamed with Divine love, will produce more good than a hundred sermons composed by a learned divine, who has but little love for God." "I will always repeat," says St. Francis de Sales, "that whoever preaches with love preaches sufficiently against heresy, although he may not utter a single word of controversy. During the thirty-three years that I have been in the ministry, I have always remarked that the practical sermons of a priest whose heart is filled with piety and zeal, are like so many burning coals heaped upon the heads of the enemies of our holy Faith. Such sermons always edify and conciliate non-Catholics."

Now it is not in the study of books, but in holy prayer and meditation, that the heart of the priest becomes enkindled with Divine love, and zeal for souls. "St. Philip Neri," says St. Alphonsus, "received far more light in the catacombs of Rome, where he spent whole nights in prayer, than in all the books which he studied; and St. Jerome acquired far greater wisdom by his meditations in the cave of Bethlehem, than by all his studies. It often happens that you learn more in one moment of prayer than in a ten-years' study. Now the more ardently we love God, the greater will be our knowledge of Him. It takes much time and labor to acquire profane sciences; but to acquire the science of the saints—the love of God—it suffices to will it earnestly, and to ask it perseveringly of God. The wise man says: 'Wisdom is easily seen by them that love her, and is found by them that seek her. She anticipateth them that covet her, so that she first showeth herself unto them. He that awaketh early to seek her shall not labor, for he finds her sitting at his door!' (*Wis.* 6:13, 16). This wisdom or love of God, as St. James the Apostle assures us (*James* 5:15-16), must be sought for in prayer."

St. Paulinus reproached Jovian, a Christian philosopher, for spending so much time in studying the works of philosophy, whilst he neglected to advance in virtue. Jovian excused himself by saying that he had no time left for prayer. "You find time," said Paulinus, "to devote to philosophy, and you find none to devote to a Christian life."

There are many students who imitate Jovian; they spend almost all their time in studying mathematics, astronomy, profane history, philosophy, and the like; and when blamed for this, they excuse themselves by saying that they have no time left for prayer and meditation. What a delusion! They find time to become learned, and they can find no time to prepare themselves for the worthy reception of Holy Orders. Seneca uttered a great truth, when he said: "We do not know what is necessary, because we learn what is superfluous." (*De Brev. Int.* ch. 1). Most assuredly it would be much better for a student to give up studying, than to let his studies interfere with his spiritual progress.

The Apostles had received the command to preach the Gospel to all nations; and though they knew that preaching was of the highest importance, nevertheless they looked upon prayer as even more important still. When they saw that their occupations became too numerous, and interfered with the sacred duty of prayer, they chose seven deacons to help them in their labors. "But," said they, "we will give ourselves continually to prayer, and to the ministry of the word." (*Acts* 6:4). They say, expressly, we must give ourselves *first* to prayer, and *then* only to the preaching of the word of God; for they knew very well that their preaching would be fruitless, unless it was accompanied by fervent prayer. St. Teresa wrote as follows, in answer to a letter of the Bishop of Osma, who, through over-great zeal for his flock, gave but little time to prayer and meditation: "Our Lord gives me to understand that you need what is most necessary—prayer and meditation, and perseverance therein; this is the cause of the dryness of your heart." St. Bernard, too, advised Pope Eugenius never to omit prayer for the sake of exterior occupations, as otherwise his heart might become so hardened as not even to heed any longer the voice of his conscience.

Whenever St. Ignatius found that a student could not apply himself to his studies with calmness of heart, and that these studies were an obstacle to his advancement in perfection, he usually took him away from them, and made him apply himself exclusively to prayer and meditation. "It may be," said he, "that he is well able to study, but study will be hurtful to him. What does it profit a man if he gaineth the whole world, but cometh to suffer the loss of his soul?" (*Life,* by C. Genelli).

St. Charles Borromeo made it a rule that a candidate for the priesthood should be asked in particular, before his ordination, whether he was in the habit of making his meditation, and in what manner he made it; and Father Avila, S.J., dissuaded everyone from becoming a priest who was not given to prayer.

Indeed, a student who is not fond of meditation and prayer will never be a good, holy priest. Woe to such a one, if during the course of his studies he has not always preferred prayer to all his other occupations! His heart will be like a hard, barren rock. Experience teaches that there is nothing which dries up the heart more quickly than study which is not sanctified by prayer. The heart of such a student will be like a reservoir that has a larger outlet than inlet. The dry land will soon make its appearance. Being destitute of interior lights, he will not see the necessity of sanctifying himself, nor the strict obligation he has to sanctify his fellow men. As he cannot have a lively faith, his genuflections at the altar, when he becomes a priest, will be like the bows of an automaton. Could you see his interior dispositions whilst celebrating the august Sacrifice of the Mass, or whilst administering the Sacraments, or reciting the Divine Office, you might be tempted to believe that you saw an actor on the stage, or a harlequin going through his role. His sermons, and all his actions, will be lifeless and mechanical.

But there is no need of heaping proofs on proofs. I will merely repeat, in conclusion, what I have said before, that a student who does not practice prayer and meditation during the course of his studies, will be unfit for ordination; and will, if he becomes a priest, not only lose his own soul, but cause the ruin of thousands of others.

Chapter 6

ON THE EFFICACY OF
THE PRAYERS OF THE JUST

My dear reader, were I to ask you whether there be any power in the world to which God Himself submits, most undoubtedly you would answer: "No, there is not, and to maintain the contrary is to incur the guilt of heresy and blasphemy." Nevertheless, I dare assert, without the slightest fear of committing the sin either of heresy or of blasphemy, that there is a power to which Almighty God Himself submits. What, then, is this power, you will eagerly ask. It is the power of the prayers of the just. Innumerable passages in Holy Writ, and in the lives of the saints, prove this great truth. I have selected several for this chapter, in the hope that you will find them interesting, and calculated to inflame your heart with still greater love for prayer.

We read in Exodus that the Jews, notwithstanding the astounding miracles which God had wrought in their behalf, when freeing them from the galling yoke of Egyptian tyranny, had fallen into the most heinous crime of idolatry. (*Ex.* 32). Exasperated at this most provoking offence, the Lord resolved to blot out this ungrateful people from the face of the earth. He was on the point of pouring out His wrath upon them, when Moses, the holy and faithful servant of God, the leader of the Israelites, interceded for them, and, by dint of earnest entreaty, arrested the arm of God uplifted to smite this ungrateful people. "Let me alone," said the Lord to Moses, "that my wrath may be enkindled against them, and that I may destroy them." (*Ex.* 32:10).

Behold the struggle between an angry God and His suppliant servant; between justice and prayer. "Let me alone," says the Lord, "let me destroy this ungrateful people, and I will make thee the leader of a great nation." Now as St. Jerome remarks, "he who says to another: 'Let me alone,' evidently shows that he is subject to the power of another." (*In Ezech.,* Chap. 13).

But Moses would not yield; on the contrary, he confidently entreated the Lord to pardon the Jews: "Why, O Lord," he asked, "is thy indignation aroused against thy people whom thou hast brought out of the land of Egypt, with great power and with a mighty hand? Let not the Egyptians boast, I beseech thee: He craftily brought them out, that he might kill them in the mountains and efface them from the earth: let thy anger cease, and be appeased upon the waywardness of thy people." (*Ex.* 32:11-12). Now what was the issue of this struggle between the justice of God and the confident prayer of Moses; for "the Lord was appeased," says Holy Scripture, "and did not the evil which he had spoken against his people." (*Ex.* 32:14).

Something similar took place at the time of the Prophet Jeremias. Again the Jews had committed atrocious crimes, and the wrath of the Lord was enkindled anew. Again He resolved to reject and destroy them: "And I will cast you away from before my face, as I have cast away all your brethren." (*Jer.* 7:15). Before inflicting this punishment, the Lord entreated His servant Jeremias not to intercede in behalf of the victims of His just indignation. "Therefore do not thou pray for this people, nor take unto thee praise and supplication for them, and *do not withstand me" (Jer.* 7:16); for if thou dost, the Lord means to say, I shall not be able to pour out My wrath upon this people.

Again, God visited this perverse people with a destructive fire in punishment of their sins. Great, indeed, must have been the anger of God to send this frightful plague; yet still greater was the power of Aaron's prayer, since it prevailed on the Lord to quench the fire instantly. Moses said to Aaron: "Take the censer, and putting fire in it from the altar, put incense upon it, and go quickly to the people to pray for them, for already wrath is gone out from the Lord, and the plague rageth." (*Num.* 16:46). And Aaron "the blameless man," says Holy Writ, "made haste to pray for the people, bringing forth the shield of his ministry—prayer—and by incense making supplication, *withstood the wrath and put an end to the calamity, showing that he was thy servant." (Wis.* 18:21). Thus Aaron checked this devouring flame, which had already consumed fourteen thousand and seventy men; he checked it not indeed by water, but by placing himself between the living and the dead, offering fervent prayer to the Lord. "And standing between the dead and the living, he prayed for the people, and the plague ceased." (*Num.* 16:48).

We read in the Book of Ecclesiasticus that God, on account of the prayer of Noah, put an end to the deluge, and saved in him and his family the whole human race. "Noah was found perfect, just." Hence it was that he could appease the wrath of God: "And in the time of wrath, he was made a reconciliation." (*Ecclus.* 44:17).

What made Attila, the scourge of God, retreat so suddenly, and give up his plan of invading Italy? It was the prayer of the Pope St. Leo, in deference to which God sent so great a consternation upon Attila, that he felt himself forced to withdraw. What put an effectual check to the ravages of pestilence at the time of St. Gregory? It was the fervent prayer of this saint. Do we not come across similar examples in almost all the lives of the saints? The hands of God are, then, so to speak, bound by the prayer of men of great sanctity; but God feels free to act, if such men cannot be found. He Himself has declared by the prophet Ezechiel: "And I sought among them a man that might set up a hedge and stand in the gap before me in favor of the land, that I might not destroy it; and I found none. And I poured out my indignation upon them; in the fire of my wrath I consumed them." (*Ezech.* 22:30-31).

The terrible fate of Sodom, as related in the Book of Genesis, is an evident proof of this truth. No sooner had Abraham learned that God intended to destroy this city with its inhabitants, than he commenced to intercede for it, saying to the Lord: "Wilt thou destroy the just with the wicked? If there be fifty just men in the city, shall they perish withal? And wilt thou not spare that place for the sake of the fifty just, if they be therein? Far be it from thee to do this thing, and to slay the just as the wicked, and for the just to be in like case as the wicked, this is not beseeming thee: thou who judgest all the earth, wilt not make this judgment.

"And the Lord said to him: If I find in Sodom fifty within the city, I will spare the whole place for their sake. And Abraham answered and said: Seeing I have once begun, I will speak to my Lord, whereas I am but dust and ashes. What if there be five less than fifty just persons? Wilt thou for five and forty destroy the whole city? And he said: I will not destroy it if I find five and forty. And again he said to him: But if forty be found there, what wilt thou do? He said: I will not destroy it for the sake of forty. Lord, saith he, be not angry, I beseech thee, if I speak: What if thirty shall be found there? He answered: I will not do it if I find thirty there. Seeing, saith he, I have once begun, I will speak to my Lord: What if twenty be found there? He said: I will not destroy it for the sake of twenty. I beseech thee, saith he, be not angry, Lord, if I speak yet once more: What if ten should be found there? And he said, I will not destroy it for the sake of ten." (*Gen.* 18:23-32).

And the Lord departed, fearing, as it were, Abraham might ask Him to spare the city if but four, or three, or even one just soul could be found there; for there was that number to be found there, viz.: Lot, his wife, and two children. But in order that Lot and his family might not perish with the rest, God, through the ministry of His angels, led them out of the city. But had the Lord found there but ten just men, surely He would have spared the city. Nay, at the time of Jeremias God declared, through this prophet, that He would be propitious to the city of Jerusalem, if but one man eminently just could be found therein. "Go about through the streets of Jerusalem and see, and consider, and seek in the broad places thereof, if you can find a man that executeth judgment and seeketh faith, *and I will be merciful unto it.*" (*Jer.* 5:1). God seeks men to whom may be applied what is said of St. John the Baptist: "He was great before the Lord"; that is, great with God by holiness of life, and by the power of prayer.

Such was St. Athanasius, who for God and for the sake of religion opposed the dreadful heresy of Arius, and triumphed over it. Such were St. John Chrysostom, St. Basil, St. Augustine, St. Ambrose, who, to the end of their lives, fought the battles of the Lord. In what great esteem must the just be held, though despicable and wretched exteriorly, because, for their sake, God spares whole cities sunk in vice; they are the stays and pillars of realms. Such was David, of whom God said to Ezechias: "I will protect this city, and will save it for my own sake, and *for David, my servant's sake.*" (*4 Kings* 19:34).

Such was St. Paul, to whom, when in danger of shipwreck, the angel of the Lord said: "Fear not, Paul, for thou must be brought before Caesar; and behold, God hath given thee all that sail with thee." (*Acts* 32:24). "God," says Cornelius à Lapide, "values one just man more than a thousand sinners, than Heaven and earth"; "Nay," says St. Alphonsus, "God esteems one eminently just man more than a thousand ordinary just men. As one sun imparts more light and warmth to the whole world than all the stars united, in like manner a holy man benefits the world more than a thousand ordinary just men." "Who will call into doubt that the world is sustained by the prayers of the saints," says Ruffinus, *(Praefat. in vit. Patr.).*

"Oh," says St. Gregory, "how I am grieved to the very heart when I see that God banishes holy men and women from one country into another, or summons them to Himself! This is to me an evident sign that He intends to punish such a country, and this will be, indeed, very easy for Him, when there is no one left to stay His anger." "The prayer of the just man," says St. Augustine, "is a key to Heaven; let his prayer ascend to Heaven, and God's mercy will descend on earth." (*Serm.* 226, *de Tempore*).

All the just of the Old and of the New Testaments employed this key of prayer very freely, to unlock God's inexhaustible treasures, and to obtain for themselves and for others whatever blessing they needed, whether temporal or spiritual. With this key the prophet Elias closed the heavens, and no rain fell for three years and a half; and with this same key he opened the heavens again, and again rain fell in abundance. With this key Ezechias brought back the shadow of the lines, by which it was gone down in the sundial of Achaz with the sun, ten lines backwards: "And the sun returned ten lines by the degrees by which it was gone down." (*Is.* 38:8).

With this key, also, Josue arrested the sun in its course, to have a longer day for gaining a complete victory over the Amorrhites: "Move not, O sun, toward Gabaon, nor thou, O moon, toward the valley of Ajalon!" (*Jos.* 10:12). What happened? "And the sun and the moon stood still, till the people revenged themselves of their enemies. So the sun stood still in the midst of Heaven, and hastened not to go down the space of one day. There was not before nor after so long a day, *the Lord obeying the voice of a man.*" (*Jos.* 10:13-14). Thus Josue exercises power over the heavenly planets, suspending their revolutions, as if king thereof, and keeping them at his will.

With the key of prayer Jacob, the Nisibite, keeps the gates of Nisibis closed against Sapor, and sets all his schemes at naught, as Theodore writes in this abbott's life; Bessarion the Abbot turns sea water into sweet water; St. Raymond of Pennafort, standing on his mantle, traverses the sea for a distance of one hundred and sixty miles; the monk Publius prevents Azazel, Julian the Apostate's devil (dispatched by this impious emperor to bring news from the West, as is related in *Vitis Pat. Lib.* 6, Tome 2, No. 12), from proceeding farther westward than where he himself lived; St. Hilarion, Macarius, and other saints drive out the devil from possessed persons; Theonas the Abbot makes robbers stand immovable; St. Gregory Thaumaturgus moves a mountain to obtain a site for a church; St. Francis of Assisi renders a wolf quite tame and gentle; St. Alphonsus stems a lava torrent of Mount Vesuvius, and turns its destructive course from the city of Naples; St. Stanislaus the Martyr restores a man to life who had died three years before, and presents him before the court to testify that he had bought from him a certain piece of ground for his church, and that he had paid him in full.

"My dear Lord," says St. Colletta, after the death of her

prior, "give me back my prior, for I need his aid still in erecting some more convents"; and Our Lord is pleased to restore this saint—her prior—alive; and he rendered her valuable services during the fifteen years he lived afterwards.

St. Francis de Paul, learning that his parents were to be executed for the supposed murder of a man whose body had been found in their garden, says to Our Lord: "My God, let me be with my parents by tomorrow." In the same night he was carried by an angel to his parents, at a distance of four hundred leagues. The next day he commands the dead man, in the presence of the people, to declare whether the murder had been justly laid to the charge of his parents. "No," says he, "your parents are guiltless." The saint again says to the Lord: "Lord, return me to my monastery"; and the angel bore him back again.

Ah, how powerful is the prayer of the just! It not only exercises its power over all kinds of creatures, rational and irrational; over those in Heaven, on earth and under the earth; it not only disarms the wrath of God against entire nations, lost to the fear and love of their Creator; it exercises even a mightier sway; it gives free access to the spiritual treasures of God; it causes them to flow in perpetual streams upon sinners, as well as upon the just, and to operate wonderful changes in their souls. Prayer, as we have seen, changes sinners from enemies of God into His friends; from reprobates into chosen vessels of election; from children of the devil into children of God; from heirs of Hell into heirs of Heaven.

Now, if prayer opens to sinners the road to Heaven, if it produces such wonderful effects in their souls, how much more wonderful are the transformations which it brings about in the souls of the just? To give a full and accurate description of them is utterly impossible; no human eye ever saw them, nor did any human understanding ever fully comprehend them. Could they be seen or understood, the whole world would covet them, and regard all else as vanity, and unworthy of man's ambition.

Now let me enumerate some of these wonderful effects of prayer. Many are the evil tendencies from which the sacred waters of Baptism do not free the soul, and many are the blemishes which still tarnish the soul, ever after the remission of grievous sins in the Sacrament of Penance; there remain, for the soul, temporal punishments to be cancelled; there remain in the soul a certain lassitude, inconstancy and discouragement in combating the temptations of the devil, of the world and of the flesh; there remain in her a certain proneness to and affection for the vanities of the world, a sovereign horror for suffering, for contempt, and the like. Now prayer removes these blemishes from the soul in proportion as she gives herself up to this holy exercise. "Although we may be filled with sins," says St. John Chrysostom, "yet, if we continue to pray, we shall soon be quite free from them"; that is to say, not only free of sins themselves, but also of the temporal punishments due to them; "for," continues the saint, "no sooner had the leper prostrated himself at the feet of Our Lord, than he was perfectly cleansed from his leprosy."

In prayer God enlightens the soul. He shows her how good He has always been to her, and how wicked she was toward Him. Seeing this goodness of God, and her own ingratitude toward Him, the soul begins to repent more perfectly. If, in the first instant of her conversion, she repented from the imperfect motive of having deserved Hell, she now begins to repent rather from the motive of the love of God. She weeps over her sins; she conceives a great hatred of the least sin, she will even shudder at the very name of sin—she feels penetrated with the spirit of penance, and is ready to accept any kind of trouble and hardship, thereby to satisfy the justice of God. Now St. Ambrose assures us that, "if the love of God has once entered into the soul, it is like a fire that destroys everything that comes within its reach; the love of God effaces every spot and stain of sin in the soul." Witness the good thief on the cross, who heard these consoling words from the lips of Our Lord, as a response to his earnest petition: "Today thou shalt be with Me in Paradise."

Moreover, prayer inspires the soul with courage to combat all her enemies, and patiently to endure every cross and trial. From being weak, she becomes strong; from being indolent and slothful, she becomes fervent and enterprising; from being perplexed, she becomes enlightened; from being melancholy and cast down, she becomes joyful; from being effeminate, she becomes manful. It is from the tower of prayer that Esther comes forth courageous to brave the orders of Assuerus; Judith to face Holofernes; a small number of the Machabees to set their numerous enemies at defiance. Fortified by prayer, Our Lord Jesus Christ goes to meet His enemies who are to crucify Him.

In prayer the soul is raised above herself, to her God in Heaven, where she sees the vanity of all earthly things, and despises them as mere trifles. There it discovers that only in Heaven, true riches, honors, and pleasures are to be found. "If we give ourselves up to prayer," says St. John Chrysostom, "we shall soon cease to be mortals, not, indeed, by nature, but by our manner of thinking, speaking, and acting, which will be Divine, having, as it were, already passed to eternal life; for those who enter into familiarity with God, must necessarily become raised above everything transitory and perishable." And: "How great a dignity is it not," continues the saint, "to be allowed to converse with God. By prayer we are united to the angelic choirs, who, lost in the contemplation of God, teach us how to forget ourselves whilst at prayer, so that, being penetrated with seraphic happiness and reverential awe at the same time, we may be lost to everything earthly, believing ourselves standing in the midst of the angels, and offering, with them, the same sacrifice. How great is the wisdom, how great the piety, how great the holiness, how great the temperance with which prayer fills us! Hence it is not the slightest deviation from truth to maintain that prayer is the source of all virtues; so much so that nothing tending to nourish piety can enter the soul without its practice." (*Lib. 2, De Orando*).

In prayer the soul is enlightened as to how all the crosses and sufferings of this world, poverty, sickness, hunger and thirst, privations of all kinds, persecutions, contempt, mockeries, insults, and whatever may be repugnant to human nature, are to be counted as nothing; and, according to St. Paul, "are not worthy to be compared with the glory to come, that shall be revealed in us." (*Rom. 8:18*). In prayer it is that she learns to exclaim with St. Andrew, the Apostle: "Oh, thou good cross, which hast received thy splendor from the members of Jesus Christ, for which I have been sighing so long, which I have always loved so ardently, and which finally has been prepared for me, oh, come and present me to my Master, so that He may receive me by thee, who by thee redeemed me!"

Hence we read that the first Christians and many martyrs suffered with joy the loss of all their temporal goods, even life itself. One day one of our fathers took dinner with an old venerable priest; whilst sitting at table, he noticed protuberances of flesh on each side of the aged priest's hands. Not knowing how to account for them, he asked him for an explanation. The venerable priest explained to him as follows: "When the slaughter of priests," said he, "was going on by wholesale, during the French

Revolution, I tried to escape death by hiding myself in a rack of hay; but I was discovered by an officer, who came and probed the rack with his sword, and pierced my hands, which were lying crosswise. I was taken to prison, to be executed on the next day. Never in my life did I experience such agony, such deadly fear; never did I understand more clearly what our dear Lord suffered in the garden of Gethsemani, than I did at that time. According to the example of my Divine Redeemer, I commenced to pray, and prayed until three o'clock in the morning. Suddenly I felt so great a comfort, consolation, and courage, that I even sighed after the hour of my execution. 'Would to God they would come!' I exclaimed, with a sigh. 'Would to God they would come!' At last the door of the prison was thrown open. 'There they are,' I said; 'thanks be to God, now I am going to die for Jesus Christ.' But, alas! My exceedingly great joy was in an instant changed into an excess of grief. I was told that I was not to be executed, but set at liberty." Thus, prayer changed this priest's sadness into joy, his cowardice into intrepidity, his horror of torture into a longing desire for the most exquisite torments.

Prayer, moreover, unites the soul to God in a most wonderful manner. This union is much stronger, more solid, more intimate, than the best kind of cement is capable of producing between two stones. Physical force can separate the latter; the former is incapable of dissolution by any natural power whatever. "He who is joined to the Lord," says St. Paul, "is one spirit." (*1 Cor.* 6:17). To be given up to prayer, and to be joined to God, is one and the same thing.

As one who frequently enjoys the company of a wise, prudent, and learned man, whom he truly loves and esteems, will, by degrees, adopt his manner and his way of speaking, judging, and acting, so a soul which converses often and long with God in prayer, will gradually receive more and more of His Divine attributes. "She will feel so strongly united to God," says St. Bernard, "that she wishes only what God wishes; nay, her will is so disposed that it cannot wish except what God wishes; but to wish what God wishes is already to be like unto God. Now not to be able to will anything save what God wills, is to be what God is, with whom to will and to be is but one and the same. Hence it is said, with truth, that we shall see Him then such as He is. Now, if we have thus become like unto Him, we shall be what He Himself is; for to whomsoever power is given to become the children of God, power is also given, not indeed to be God themselves, but to be what God is." (*St. Bern.* or *Auct. Tract. De Vita Solitar.*).

Hence, St. Francis of Assisi, when at prayer, was often-times rapt in ecstasy, and, regardless of earth and the love of created things, he would exclaim, in a transport of delight: "My God and my All! My God and my All! Let me die for the love of Thee, Who hast died for the love of me!"

Hence that brilliant light ever beaming on the counte-nances of holy men when returning from fervent prayer and familiar intercourse with God. "And when Moses came down from Mount Sinai . . . he knew not that his face was horned, from the conversation of the Lord." (*Ex.* 34:29).

Those who are devoted to prayer and frequent conver-sation with God become like unto Moses, whose brow was resplendent with a supernatural light. This brilliancy is first visible on their countenance, from whence it extends to the whole body. Thus Jesus Christ was transfigured in prayer, and His face did shine as the sun; so much so, that this light was not only reflected upon Moses and Elias, but also upon St. Peter, St. James, and St. John, in which light St. Peter, inebriated with joy, exclaims: "Lord, it is good for us to be here, if Thou wilt let us make here three tabernacles; one for Thee, and one for Moses, and one for Elias."

Thus also the face of St. Anthony, who often spent whole nights in prayer, was resplendent to such a degree that by the splendor, radiance, and joy on his countenance, he could be recognized at once among many thousands of his brethren, like a sun among many stars. Thus, too, St. Francis of Assisi, whilst elevated in spirit to Heaven in the act of fervent prayer, was radiant with light, and seemed to send forth fiery flames. In the Breviary, we read that the face of St. Stanislaus Koska was always inflamed, nay, sometimes, even beaming, with Divine light.

Thus, also, the countenance of the Blessed Virgin Mary shone constantly, and in an especial manner, with heavenly light, on account of her perpetual union with God and the Incarnate Word; and such was its dazzling splendor, that, according to the testimony of St. Dionysius the Areopagite, she seemed to be a goddess.

Now these beams radiated in the shape of horns, to signify that the saints were not only enlightened in prayer, but became also *cornuti; i.e.* horned; namely, constant, firm, strong, intrepid, and capable of undergoing every suffering, and of enduring all kinds of hardships.

Thus Anna, the mother of Samuel, felt great strength and courage after her prayer. "And her countenance," says Holy Writ, "was no more changed" (*1 Kings* 1:18); that is, she obtained such strength in prayer that she bore with an even mind both the praises of Helcana and the contempt and mockery of Phenanna; consolations and prosperity, as well as desolations and adversities.

Finally, prayer introduces the soul into the happy country of the interior life, a country that overflows with milk and honey. Here the soul learns more of God in one moment, than by reading all the books in the world; God speaks to the soul, and the soul to God, in an inexplicable manner, enkindling in her that strong, ardent, and seraphic love for Himself, which made St. Paul exclaim: "Who, then, shall separate us from the love of Christ? Shall tribulations? or distress? or famine? or nakedness? or danger? or persecution? or the sword? (As it is written: For thy sake we are put to death all the day long: we are accounted as sheep for the slaughter.)" (*Rom.* 8:35-36). "Even unto this hour we both hunger and thirst, and are naked, and are buffeted, and have no fixed abode. We are reviled. . . . we are persecuted . . . we are blasphemed; we are made as the refuse of this world, the off-scouring of all, even until now." (*1 Cor.* 4:11-13). "Our flesh had no rest, but we suffered all tribulation; combats without, fears within." (*2 Cor.* 7:5).

"In many labors, in prisons more frequently, in stripes above measure, in deaths often. Of the Jews, five times did I receive forty stripes, save one. Thrice was I beaten with rods, once I was stoned, thrice I suffered shipwreck; a night and a day I was in the depth of the sea. In journeying often, in perils of water, in perils of robbers, in perils from my own nation, in perils from the Gentiles, in perils in the city, in perils in the wilderness, in perils in the sea, in perils from false brethren. In labor and painfulness, in much watchings, in hunger and thirst, in fastings often, in cold and in nakedness." (*2 Cor.* 11:23-27). "We glory in tribulations." (*Rom.* 5:3). "I am filled with comfort; I exceedingly abound with joy in our tribulation." (*2 Cor.* 7:4). "In all these things we overcome, because of him that hath loved us. For I am sure that neither death, nor life, nor angels, nor principalities, nor powers, nor things present, nor things to come, nor might, nor height, nor depth, nor any other creature, shall be able to separate us from the love of God, which is in Christ Jesus our Lord." (*Rom.* 8:37-39).

What is there, then, that cannot be obtained through prayer? "All things whatsoever you shall ask in prayer, believing, you shall receive." (*Matt.* 21:22). Now, He who says all things, excepts nothing. Nay, God is so good, so liberal, says Origen (*Hom.* 9, *in Numer.*) that He gives more than He is asked for. The Holy Church, too, expresses this when she prays: "O God, Who, in the abundance of Thy kindness, *exceedest both the merits and wishes of Thy suppliants,* pour forth upon us Thy mercy, that Thou mayest free us from those things which burden our conscience, and mayest grant us what we dare not ask."

Let us rest assured that he who understands how to pray well becomes, as it were, the lord of the Lord, and the ruler of the universe. He is another Jacob, who, having overcome the Lord in wrestling (in prayer), was called Israel, that is, the conqueror of God. "If you can" says Cornelius à Lapide, "reason with God effectually in prayer, He will change your enemies at once into your friends; for the hearts even of the most ferocious are in the hands of the Lord; He can change them at His own good pleasure." "If thou hast been strong against God, how much more shalt thou prevail against men!" (*Gen.* 32:28). Indeed, whomsoever the Creator Himself obeys, the angels, the demons, men, and all creatures, are bound to obey.

Chapter 7

ON THE POWER OF
THE PRAYER OF CHILDREN

Once the Emperor Henry besieged a certain city for a considerable time. The inhabitants were unwilling to surrender; so he notified them that he would give orders to his soldiers to take the city by assault, and massacre all its inhabitants to a man, even the little children. Alarmed at this proclamation, and seeing no hope left of saving themselves except in moving the Emperor to compassion, the inhabitants of the city had recourse to the following means. They collected all the little children from six to ten years of age, and after having arrayed them in procession, they made them march before the Emperor, and throw themselves on their knees, strike their breasts, and cry aloud in pitiful accents: *"Have pity on us, O Emperor! O Emperor, have pity on us!"* This heart-rending scene affected the Emperor so much that he could not help weeping himself. He pardoned the inhabitants of the city, and raised the siege immediately.

If the prayer of a child is so powerful with man, it is far more so with God. The prayers of children will sometimes move God, when the prayers of others will not move Him.

We read in Holy Scripture that Agar was wandering in the sandy deserts of Arabia with her little boy, Ismael. She had with her a bottle of water for him to drink. There was no other water in the deserts. When the water in the bottle was finished, she put the little boy under one of the trees and went a great way off from him; for, she said, I will not see the boy die of thirst. Then she sat down and lifted up her voice, and began to cry for the poor dying boy. Then an angel of God called to Agar from Heaven, and said: "What art thou doing, Agar? fear not, *for God hath heard the voice of the boy.* Arise, take up the boy! . . . And God opened her eyes, and she saw a well of water, and went and filled the bottle and gave the boy to drink." (*Gen.* 21:17-19). So God heard the voice, *not of the mother, but of the child,* and He gave them water to drink. So God hears the prayers of children.

There is a feeling common to all people that the prayer of children is all-powerful with God. We know this from the revelation of God Himself: "Out of the mouths of infants thou hast perfected praise." (*Ps.* 8:3).

There was a town called Bethulia. One day the church there was full of children. What was the matter? The soldiers were on their road to this town. They were coming to kill the people. The people knew that God hears the prayers of children; for they had read in the Holy Scriptures, *"out of the mouths of infants come forth perfect praise of God."* So they made all the children come into the church and bow their heads down to the ground, and pray for the people. God heard the prayers of the children. He made the cruel soldiers go away, and the people were saved by the prayers of the children.

Dear little child, if you have parents who do not lead a good life, God looks to you for their conversion. But what can you do? The good example of a child speaks to the heart of a parent. Then there is prayer—will God turn a deaf ear to the prayer of a child praying for the conversion of its father or mother? No; the Hail Mary which you say every day for their conversion, the prayer you say for them each time you hear Mass, the Holy Communions you offer for them, the sighs of your heart, all rise up before God, and are not forgotten by Him; and the day will come when God will send down from Heaven the grace of conversion into the hearts of your parents.

During one of our missions, a certain child knelt down every night to say three Our Fathers and three Hail Marys for the conversion of his father. One night, toward the end of the mission, when the child was again kneeling down and praying, the father said: "Child, what are you doing there?" "Father," replied the child, "I am praying for your conversion." In this moment the father felt touched by the grace of God. Next day he went to church, made a good confession, and was reconciled with God. Thus it was by the prayer of this good child that God was moved to bestow the grace of conversion upon his father.

God often makes use of children to convert others. Louis Veuillot, editor of the *L'Universe* in Paris, gave the following account of his conversion: "I had been brought up," he said, "in ignorance of the truth, with no respect for religion, and hating the Catholic Church. I had a little child, which was wild, passionate, and stupid. I was cross and severe to this child. Sometimes my wife used to say to me: 'Wait a little, the child will be better when it makes its First Communion.' I did not believe it. However, the child began to go to catechism. From that time it became obedient, respectful, and affectionate. I thought I would go myself to hear the instructions on the catechism, which had made such a wonderful change in my child. I went, and I heard truths which I had never heard before. My feelings toward the child were changed. It was not so much love as respect I began to feel for the child. I was inferior to it. It was better and wiser than I was. The week for the First Communion was come. There were but five or six days remaining. One morning the child returned from Mass, and came into a room where I was alone. 'Father,' said the child, 'the day of my First Communion is coming. I cannot go to the altar without asking your blessing, and forgiveness for all the faults I have committed and the pain I have often given you. Think well of my faults, and scold me for them all, that I may commit them no more.' 'My child,' I answered, 'A father forgives everything.' The child looked at me with tears in its eyes, and threw its arms round my neck. 'Father,' said the child again, 'I have something else to ask you.' I knew well—my conscience told me—what the child was going to ask; I was afraid, and said: 'Go away now, you can ask me tomorrow.'

"The poor child did not know what to say, so it left me, and went sorrowfully into its own little room, where it had an altar with an image of the Blessed Virgin upon it. I felt sorry for what I had said; so I got up and walked softly on the tips of my feet to the room-door of my child. The door was a little open; I looked at the child; it was on its knees before the Blessed Virgin, *praying with all its heart for its father*. Truly, at that moment I knew what one must feel at the sight of an angel. I went back to my room, and leaned my head on my hands; I was ready to cry. I heard a slight sound, and raised my eyes—my child was standing before me; on its face there was fear, with firmness and love. 'Father,' said the child, 'I cannot put off till tomorrow what I have to ask you—I ask you, on the day of my First Communion, to come to the Holy Communion along with mamma and me.' I burst into tears, and threw my arms round the child's neck, and said: 'Yes, my child, yes, this very day you shall take me by the hand and lead me to your confessor, and say: "Here is father."'" So this child also obtained, by its prayer, the grace of conversion for its father.

You may ask why is it that the prayer of little children is so powerful with God? It is because they are innocent, and God willingly hears the prayer of an innocent heart. When our dear Saviour lived on earth, He embraced the little children; He laid His hands upon them, and He blessed them. He rebuked those who tried to prevent little children from being presented to Him, that He might bless them. He said: "Suffer the little children to come unto me, and forbid them not: for of such is the kingdom of God." (*Mark* 10:14). Now children go to Jesus, if they pray to Jesus; and Jesus never lets them go away without having blessed them; that is to say, without having heard their prayers.

Chapter 8

ON THE CONDITIONS AND
QUALITIES OF PRAYER

Plutarch relates that, in his time, the Romans sent a delegation of three men to Bithynia, in order to restore peace between a father and his son. One of the delegates had his head covered with ulcers; the other suffered from gout, and the third from heart disease. When Cato, the Roman Censor, saw them, he exclaimed: "This Roman delegation has neither head, nor foot, nor heart!" I fear, dear reader, that we often send similarly worthless delegations to God. Our delegate to Him is prayer, of which David has said: "Let my prayer come before thee" (*Ps.* 87:3), on which words St. Augustine comments thus: "Oh, wonderful power of prayer, which has access to God, whilst the flesh is refused admittance!" Now in order that prayer, our delegate, may please God, and prove as useful and powerful to us as it has to the saints, it must have certain conditions and qualities, which I will now proceed to unfold.

I. *The Object of our Prayer must be Lawful.*

God is our Father. Now a father will not give to his children what he knows to be hurtful to them. Should we, then, ask of our Heavenly Father something that is detrimental to us, especially to our salvation, He will not hear our prayer. The object of our prayer, then, must be lawful, and conducive to our spiritual welfare, as otherwise it would be displeasing to God; and it would be unreasonable for us to expect that God would grant us something which is displeasing to Him. Accordingly, God will not hear us:

1. If we ask for something that is detrimental to our salvation. "A man" says St. Augustine, "may lawfully pray for the goods of this life, and the Lord may mercifully refuse to hear him." As a physician who desires the restoration of his patient will not allow him those things which he knows will be hurtful to him, so, in like manner, the Lord will turn a deaf ear to your prayers when you ask for such things as He knows will be detrimental to you. It is not forbidden, however, to pray for the necessaries of this life: "Give me only the necessaries of life" (*Prov.* 30:8); nor is it wrong to be solicitous about such things, provided our anxiety with regard to them be not inordinate, and we do not set our hearts upon them so absolutely as to make them the chief objects of our desires. We must always ask for them with resignation, and on the condition that they be of advantage to our souls. We read in the life of St. Thomas of Canterbury that a sick man had recovered his health through the saint's intercession; reflecting afterwards that sickness might have been better for him than health, he prayed again to the holy bishop, saying that he would prefer being sick, if sickness was better for him than health; and immediately his sickness returned.

2. God will not hear our prayer if we pray to be delivered from a particular temptation, or cross (as St. Paul prayed for deliverance from the temptations of the flesh), which God knows to be useful to our advancement in humility and other virtues.

3. Nor will God hear us if we ask for something from motives of ambition, like the sons of Zebedee, who prayed to obtain the principal offices in the kingdom of Christ.

4. God will not hear us if we ask for something from indiscreet zeal, as the Apostles did, when they asked Our Lord to send fire from Heaven upon the Samaritans, who had rejected Christ our Saviour.

5. Nor will God hear us if we ask of Him for a certain particular state of life, as, for instance, the religious, or the matrimonial, which He knows is not suited to our physical, intellectual, and moral constitution. The best prayer we can perform in such a case is daily to beseech the Almighty to direct us by such ways and means as will preserve us from sin, make us more holy, and lead us to life everlasting, saying: "Lord, what wilt Thou have me to do?" "My heart is ready, O God, my heart is ready." "Show, O Lord, thy ways to me, and teach me thy paths." (*Ps.* 24:4). "As we know not, O Lord, what to do, we can only turn our eyes to thee." (*2 Par.* 20:12). "Guide me, O Lord, by those ways, offices, actions, exercises and sufferings, which Thou knowest will lead me most safely to Paradise, and to greater glory in Thy heavenly kingdom; or grant, O Lord, what Jesus Christ, my Redeemer Himself, wishes to see in me; and what He wills should be given to me; and what, when dying on the Cross, He asked for me." Or: "Grant me, O Lord, what the Blessed Virgin Mary asks for me; for she loves me, and wishes to see me saved, and knows best what I need to obtain eternal happiness." This is a very pious and most efficacious manner of praying.

6. God often delays hearing our prayer if the object of it is not profitable to us at the time, but is so only at a later period. One day St. Gertrude complained to Our Lord because she had not obtained from Him a certain favor for her relatives, notwithstanding the promise He had made to

her to hear all her prayers. Our Lord told her that He had heard her prayer, but would grant the favor she had asked for at some future time, when it would be more useful to her relatives.

7. If our prayers are said, as it were, at random, without asking any particular grace, they are also more or less defective, and inefficacious. "You know not what you ask" (*Mark* 10:88), said Our Lord Jesus Christ to the sons of Zebedee, when they asked of Him that they might sit, one on His right hand and the other on His left, in His glory. Alas! How many Christians are there not to whom Our Lord could address the same words: "You do not know what you ask of God." How many are there who, if they were asked on their way to church, or during their stay therein, or on their return from it, what they sought to obtain in their prayers, would be at a loss for an answer, not knowing what they need, nor what to ask for. But it is self-deception to go to the altar and ask something merely at random. This is to be like a person who is sick and goes to a druggist to buy medicine, without reflecting whether or not it will suit his particular disease. Such a manner of praying is certainly injudicious, because it is not adapted to the spiritual wants of our souls. Hence we must see that our prayers be so ordered as to correspond with our particular necessities. "When at prayer," says St. Francis de Sales, "let us be like a strong, robust, and sensible man, who, when sitting at table, takes such food as will give him bodily strength; but let us not be like children, who grasp at sweet things: such as sugar, cakes, pears, apples and the like." Prayer is called the food of the soul, but it is so only when we pray according to our spiritual wants.

8. If we pray in too general a manner; for example, should a person, from certain circumstances in life, either from necessity or otherwise, be thrown into the society of another of a quarrelsome and irritable disposition, he

would naturally desire not to lose patience, or become angry, or use uncharitable words or reproaches. Now should he pray thus to God: "Lord, give me patience, make me humble and charitable," this prayer would be rather too general and indefinite. It would be better to say: "Lord, make me patient and charitable toward this person; give me also the grace to have immediate recourse to Thee, whenever ill feelings begin to arise in my heart; at that very moment make me pray that I may have strength to resist them, for the love of Thee." It is not here intended to convey the idea that to pray in a general manner for our wants is not good, but only that it is better to pray according to the particular circumstances of our wants.

9. There is yet another mode of praying in use with many persons which is not very profitable to the soul, and is, therefore, more or less inexpedient; it is to pray by way of affections, for instance: "O excess of love! One heart is too little to love Thee, my Jesus; one tongue is not enough to praise Thy goodness. O my Jesus, how great are my obligations to Thee! No, I will no longer live in myself; but Jesus alone shall live in me; He is mine, and I am His. O love! O love! No more sins! I will never forget the goodness of God, and the mercies of my Saviour. I love Thee, O Infinite Majesty! My God, I wish to love nothing but Thee," etc.

Expressions like these are called devout affections of the heart; but as they do not contain the least petition for any particular grace, the soul will not become over-rich with the gifts of God if this manner of prayer alone be adopted. If a beggar were to say to a millionaire: "Oh, how magnificent is your house! How splendid your furniture! How elegant your grounds! How vast your wealth!" it would hardly induce the rich man to give him an alms. But should the poor man say: "My good sir, be kind enough to assist me in my poverty; please give me some money, some clothes, some provisions," etc., then the rich man, if charitably disposed, will not fail to comply with the poor man's request. In like manner Our Lord is not bound to bestow graces upon us merely because we admire His perfections, goodness, or other attributes. But if we say to Him: "Lord, make me understand better the excess of Thy love; grant that my heart may never love anything but Thee, that it may ever be Thine; make me always seek only Thee, let everything else be disgustful to me," etc.; expressions like these being petitions or prayers, in which we ask for particular graces, Our Lord Jesus Christ, on account of His promise, feels bound to grant them.

Although devout affections are good, and often quite natural to the soul, yet, generally speaking, petitions are better, far more profitable, and more conformable to the examples taught us by Our Lord Jesus Christ, the Holy Church in her authorized devotions, and all the saints. Read the prayer of Our Lord for His disciples in the Gospel of St. John (*John* 17), or any prayer of the Church, or of any saint, and the truth of this will be seen at once. Read the prayer which St. Alphonsus, who is justly termed the Apostle of Prayer, addresses to Our Lord in the Blessed Sacrament, and which commences thus: "O my Jesus, Thou Who art the True Life, make me die to the world to live only to Thee; my Redeemer, by the flames of Thy love destroy in me all that is displeasing to Thee, and give me a true desire to gratify and please Thee in all things," etc.

The venerable Paul Segneri used to say that at one time he used to employ the time of prayer in reflections and affections; "but God [these are his own words] afterwards enlightened me, and thence forward I endeavored to spend my time in making petitions; and if there is any good in me, I ascribe it to this manner of recommending myself to

God." Let us do the same. It may not be out of place to suggest that a prayerbook, in which the prayers are put up in the form of petitions, is to be most recommended.

Certain persons having heard, or read, in the lives of St. Teresa and other saints, of the grades of supernatural prayer, namely, the prayer of quiet, of sleep, or suspension of the faculties, of union, of ecstasy or rapture, of flight and impetus of the spirit, and of the wound of love, may feel anxious to possess, and even pray fervently for, these supernatural gifts. The learned and pious Palafox, Bishop of Osma, in a note on the Eighteenth Letter of St. Teresa says: "Observe that these supernatural graces, which God deigned to bestow on St. Teresa and other saints, are not necessary for the attainment of sanctity, since, without them, many have arrived at a high degree of perfection, and obtained eternal life, while many who enjoyed them were afterwards damned." He says that "the practice of the Gospel virtues, and particularly of the love of God, being the true and only way to sanctify our souls, it is superfluous, and even presumptuous, to desire and seek such extraordinary gifts." These virtues are acquired by prayer, and by corresponding with the lights and helps of God, who ardently desires our sanctification: "For this is the will of God, your sanctification." (*1 Thess.* 4:3).

Speaking of the degrees of supernatural prayer described by St. Teresa, the holy bishop wisely observes that "as to the prayer of *quiet,* we should only desire and beg of God to free us from all attachment and affection to worldly goods, which, instead of giving peace to the soul, fill it with inquietude and affliction. Solomon justly called them 'vanity of vanities, and vexation of spirit.' (*Eccles.* 1:14).

"The heart of man can never enjoy true peace till it is divested of all that is not God, and entirely devoted to His holy love to the exclusion of every other object. But man himself cannot attain to this perfect consecration of his being to God; he can only obtain it by constant prayer. As to the *sleep,* or *suspension of the powers,* we should entreat the Almighty to keep them in a profound sleep with regard to all temporal affairs, and awake only to meditate on His Divine Goodness, and to seek Divine love and eternal goods. For all sanctity, and the perfection of charity, consist in the union of our will with the holy will of God. As to *union of the powers,* we should only pray that God may teach us, by His grace, not to think of, or seek, or wish for anything but what He wills. As to *ecstasy,* or *rapture,* let us beseech the Lord to eradicate from our hearts all inordinate love of ourselves and of creatures, and to draw us entirely to Himself.

"As to the *flight of the spirit,* we should merely implore the grace of perfect detachment from the world, that, like the swallow, which never seeks its food on the earth, and even feeds in its flight, we may never fix our heart on any sensual enjoyment, but, always tending toward Heaven, employ the goods of this world only for the support of life. As to the *impulse of spirit,* let us ask of God courage and strength to do that violence to ourselves which may be necessary to resist the attacks of the enemy, to overcome our passions, or to embrace sufferings, even in the midst of spiritual dryness and desolation. Finally, as to the *wound of love,* as the remembrance of a wound is constantly kept alive by the pain it inflicts, so we should supplicate Our Lord to wound our hearts with holy love to such a degree that we may be always reminded of His goodness and affection toward us, that thus we may devote our lives to love, and please Him by our works and affections. These graces will not be obtained without prayer; but by humble, confident, and persevering prayer, all the gifts of God may be procured."

Let us, then, always pray the Lord to hear us, not, indeed, according to our will, but rather to grant us what may be conducive to our sanctification and salvation. Let us not be like the blind man in the Gospel, whom our Saviour asked, "What wilt thou that I do to thee?" (*Luke* 18:41). "Indeed," says St. Bernard, "this man was truly blind, God finding it necessary to ask him what He should do to him; he should have said: 'Lord, be it far from me that Thou shouldst do to me according to my will; no, do to me according to Thy will, and what Thou knowest is best for me.'" St. Jerome writes, in his letter to Salvian, that Nebridius was in the habit of asking of God to give him what He knew was best for him. St. John says: "This is the confidence which we have towards him, that whatsoever we shall ask, *according to his will,* he heareth us." (*1 John* 5:14).

Such was the prayer of Solomon. "And the Lord appeared to Solomon . . . saying: Ask what thou wilt that I should give thee. And Solomon said: . . . O Lord God, thou hast made thy servant king instead of David my father: and I am but a child, and know not how to go out and come in . . . Give, therefore, to thy servant an understanding heart to . . . *discern between good and evil.* And the Lord said to Solomon: Because thou hast asked this thing, and hast not asked for thyself long life, nor riches, nor the lives of thy enemies, but hast asked *for thyself wisdom to discern judgment, behold, I have done for thee according to thy words,* and have given thee a wise and understanding heart, insomuch that there hath been no one like thee before thee, nor shall arise after thee. Yea, and the things also which thou didst not ask I have given thee: to wit, riches and glory, so that no one hath been like thee among the kings in all days heretofore." (*3 Kings* 3:5ff.).

Solomon is called the "Wise Man," and indeed, he manifested great wisdom in his prayer to God; so much so that the Lord praised him for it, and granted him not only what he asked, but even far more than he could expect. Let us pray like him, saying: "Lord, I am living in a wicked world, surrounded with dangers which lead to perdition. I am like a child, not knowing how to walk on, or follow the true way. Give, therefore, to Thy servant an understanding heart to discern between good and evil. Make me understand how great an evil sin is, and how great a good it is to love Thee above all things. Give me a great hatred of sin, and make me love Thee most ardently to the end of my life."

Or let us pray like St. Francis of Assisi: "'Our Father,' most blessed, most holy, our Creator, Redeemer, and Comforter; 'Who art in Heaven,' where Thou dwellest with the angels and the saints, whom Thou enlightenest and inflamest with Thy love so that they may know Thee; for Thou, O Lord, art the life and love that dwell in them; Thou art their everlasting happiness, communicating Thyself to them; Thou art the supreme and eternal Source from which all blessings flow, and without Thee there is none. 'Hallowed be Thy name'; enlighten us with Thy Divine wisdom, that we may be able to know Thee, and to comprehend the boundless extent of Thy mercies to us, Thy everlasting promises, Thy sublime majesty, and Thy profound judgments. 'Thy kingdom come'; so that Thy grace may reign in our hearts, and prepare us for Thy heavenly kingdom, where we shall see Thee clearly, and perfectly love Thee, rejoicing with Thee and in Thee through all eternity. 'Thy will be done on earth as it is in Heaven'; that being occupied with Thee we may love Thee with our whole heart, with our whole soul, desiring nothing but Thee; with our whole mind, referring all things to Thee, and ever seeking Thy glory in all our actions; with our whole strength, employing all our faculties, both of body and soul, in Thy service, applying them to no other end whatsoever than to promote Thy Kingdom, seeking to draw all men to Thee, and to love our neighbor as ourselves, rejoicing at his welfare and happiness as if it were our own, sympathizing with his necessities and giving no offence to him. 'Give us this day our daily bread'; thy dearly beloved Son, Our Lord Jesus Christ; we ask Him of Thee as our daily bread, in order that we may be mindful of the love He testified for us, and of the things He promised, did, and suffered for us; grant us the grace always to keep them in our thoughts, and to value them exceedingly. 'Forgive us our trespasses'; through Thy unspeakable mercy, through the merits of the Passion and death of Thy most dearly beloved Son, through the intercession of the Holy Virgin Mary, and of all the saints. 'As we forgive them that trespass against us'; grant us the grace that we may sincerely and truly forgive our enemies, and pray earnestly to Thee for them; that we may never return evil for evil, but seek to do good to those who injure us. 'And lead us not into temptation,' whether it be concealed, manifest, or sudden, 'but deliver us from evil,' past, present, and future."

Let us also learn, from this prayer of the "Our Father," how pleasing it must be to God to pray for others. In this prayer Jesus Christ teaches us to pray not only for ourselves, but also for all our fellow men. He also taught us, by His example, to pray for others. Indeed, we may say that His whole life was a continual prayer for the just, as well as for sinners. "And not for them only [the Apostles] do I pray, but for them also who, through their word, shall believe in me, that they all may be one, as thou, Father, in me, and I in thee, that they also may be one in us, that the world may believe that thou hast sent me." (*John* 17:20-21).

"Pray one for another," says St. James the Apostle, "that you may be saved." (*James* 5:16). We are especially bound to pray for the successor of St. Peter, our Holy Father the Pope, for the bishops and clergy of the Holy Catholic Church, and for all those who labor for the propagation of our holy Faith. Jesus Christ Himself has given us the example. "And now I am no more in the world; and these [the Apostles] are in the world, and I come to thee. Holy Father, keep them in thy name, whom thou hast given me, that they may be one, as we also are. . . . I do not ask that thou shouldst take them away out of the world, but that thou shouldst preserve them from evil. Sanctify them in truth. . . . Father, I will that where I am, they also, whom thou hast given me, may be with me; that they may see my glory, which thou hast given me." (*John* 17:11, 15, 17, 24).

Moreover, we should often recommend to God all poor sinners, schismatics, heretics and infidels. Our Lord Jesus Christ, when hanging on the Cross and suffering the most excruciating pains, prayed for the greatest sinners and His most bitter enemies: "Father, forgive them, for they know not what they do." (*Luke* 23:34). "He that knoweth his brother to sin a sin, which is not unto death, let him ask, and life [life of grace] shall be given to him that sinneth not to death." (*1 John* 5:16).

Remarkable instances of sinners leaving their evil ways and returning to God occur every day. No doubt their conversion is owing to the prayers of the just; "For God willingly hears the prayer of a Christian," says St. John Chrysostom, "not only when he prays for himself, but also when he prays for sinners. Necessity obliges us to pray for ourselves, but charity must induce us to pray for others. The prayer of fraternal charity is more acceptable to God than that of necessity." (*Chrysost. Hom.* 14., *Oper. Imper. in Matt.*). The prayer for sinners, says St. Alphonsus, is not only beneficial to them, but is, moreover, most pleasing to God; and the Lord Himself complains of His servants who do not recommend sinners to Him. He said one day to St. Mary Magdalen of Pazzi: "See, my daughter, how the Christians are in the devil's hands; if My elect did not deliver them by their prayers, they would be devoured."

Inflamed with holy zeal by these words, this saint used to offer to God the Blood of the Redeemer fifty times a day in behalf of sinners. "Ah," she used to exclaim, "how great a pain it is, O Lord, to see how one could help Thy creatures by dying for them, and not be able to do so!" In every one of her spiritual exercises she recommended sinners to God, and it is related in her life that she scarcely spent an hour in the day without praying for them; she even frequently arose in the middle of the night to go before the Blessed Sacrament, to offer prayers for them. She went so far as to desire to endure even the pains of Hell for their conversion, provided she could still love God in that place, and God granted her wish by inflicting on her most violent pains and infirmities for the salvation of sinners; and yet after all this she shed bitter tears, thinking she did nothing for their conversion. "Ah, Lord, make me die," she often exclaimed, "and return to life again as many times as is necessary to satisfy Thy justice for them!" God, as is related in her life, did not fail to give the grace of conversion to many sinners, on account of her fervent prayers. "Souls," says St. Alphonsus, "that really love God, will never neglect to pray for poor sinners."

How could it be possible for a person who really loves God, and knows His ardent love for our souls, and how much He wishes us to pray for sinners, and how much Jesus Christ has done and suffered for their salvation; how could it be possible for such a one, I say, to behold with indifference so many poor souls deprived of God's grace without feeling moved frequently to ask God to give light and strength to these wretched beings, in order that they may come out of the miserable state of spiritual death in which they are slumbering? It is true, God has not promised to grant our petitions in behalf of those who put a positive obstacle in the way of their conversion; yet God, in His goodness, has often deigned, through the prayers of His servants, to bring back the most blind and obstinate sinners to the way of salvation, by means of extraordinary graces. Therefore we should never fail to recommend poor sinners to God in all our spiritual exercises; moreover, he who prays for others will experience that his prayers for himself will be heard much sooner. In the life of St. Margaret of Cortona, we read that she prayed more than a hundred times a day for the conversion of sinners; and, indeed, so numerous were their conversions, that the Franciscan Fathers complained to her of not being able to hear the confessions of all those who were converted by her prayers.

The Curé of Ars, who died a few years since in the odor of sanctity, relates the following in one of his catechetical instructions: "A great lady, of one of the first families in France, was here, and she went away this morning. She is rich, very rich, and scarcely twenty-three. She has offered herself to God for the conversion of sinners and the expiation of sin. She mortifies herself in a thousand ways, wears a girdle all armed with iron points, her parents know nothing of it; she is as white as a sheet of paper." (*Spirit of Curé of Ars.*).

The same saintly pastor said one day to a priest who complained of not being able to change the hearts of his parishioners for the better: "You prayed, you wept, you sighed; but did you fast also? Did you deprive yourself of sleep? Did you sleep on the bare ground? Did you scourge yourself? Do not think you have done all, if you have not yet done these penances."

If we do not love poor sinners that much, if we think it above our strength to perform similar penitential works for their conversion, let us at least do something; let us recommend them to the Sacred Hearts of Jesus and Mary, or offer ourselves for a week or two as a holocaust to God, to be disposed of according to His good pleasure; let us suffer some cold, some heat, some inconvenience, some contradiction and contempt in silence; let us deny ourselves some agreeable visits, or other natural pleasures; or let us make a novena, or hear Mass daily for a week, and offer up our Communions with this intention. We may be assured that by such exercises we shall give great pleasure to Jesus Christ, contribute much to the honor of His Heavenly Father, win His heart over to ourselves, force it sweetly to give the grace of conversion to many sinners, and obtain for ourselves a large share of Divine grace.

II. *Our Prayer must be Humble.*

"Two men went up into the temple to pray; the one a Pharisee, the other a publican. The Pharisee, standing, prayed thus to himself: O God, I give thee thanks that I am not as the rest of men, extortioners, unjust, adulterers, as also is this publican. I fast thrice in the week; I give tithes of all I possess. And the publican, standing afar off, would not so much as lift up his eyes towards heaven, but struck his breast, saying: O Lord, be merciful to me a sinner! I say to you, this man went down into his house justified, rather than the other." (*Luke* 18:10-14).

In this parable of the Pharisee and the Publican, Our Lord Jesus Christ teaches us that prayer without humility obtains nothing. As the Pharisee left the temple just as bad and as sinful as he entered, so shall we not improve by prayer, if we pray with the same sentiments of pride and self-conceit. Even common sense tells us that prayer, to be good, must be humble. Should a poor man beg alms in a haughty and impudent manner, he would be despised by every person; for to beg and to be proud at the same time is an abominable thing. All beggars know this but too well; hence many of them study different ways and manners to show themselves humble; they take the last place; they adopt humble language; they fall prostrate before you, if you meet them, asking alms with joined hands and with tears in their eyes. Should they have a good suit of clothes, they will put on ragged and tattered ones when they go out begging. How many humble reasons do they not allege to obtain an alms, such as not having eaten anything for the whole day. They pretend to suffer innumerable infirmities, and so lamentably do they sigh, as even to move the hardest hearts to pity. No one blames them for this conduct; everyone, on the contrary, approves of their manner of acting.

If humility, then, is required from men when asking a favor of their fellow men, how much more will it not be required from us by the Lord of Heaven and earth, when we address Him in prayer? To know that we are sinners, and that we have so often offended the Divine Majesty; that we have crucified Our Lord Jesus Christ by our heinous sins; to know that if God did not assist us every day we would commit most shameful crimes, and become even worse than the brute—all this should, undoubtedly, be a sufficient reason for us always to remain humble, and to pray with sentiments of exterior and interior humility, saying, with the Publican, "Lord, be merciful to me a sinner!" in order that we, like him, may always come forth from prayer more acceptable, more justified, and more sanctified in the sight of the Lord of Heaven and earth. "From the beginning have the proud not been acceptable to thee," said Judith, "but the prayer of the humble and the meek hath always pleased thee." (*Jdt.* 9:16).

How great was not the wisdom which Solomon received in prayer! But in what manner, and with what sentiments, did he pray? Holy Writ says that Solomon, when praying, "had fixed both knees on the ground, and had spread his hands towards heaven." (*3 Kings* 8:54). St. Stephen effected by his prayer the conversion of St. Paul the Apostle, and of many others of his enemies. But how humble was not his prayer? "Falling on his knees," says Holy Scripture, "he cried with a loud voice, saying: Lord, lay not this sin to their charge." (*Acts* 7:59). How humble must not have been the prayer of St. James the Apostle, who used to pray so long on his knees that the skin of them became as hard as that of a camel. St. John Chrysostom adds that also the skin of the forehead of this Apostle had become quite hard from lying with it prostrate on the ground whilst at prayer. Ribadeneira and others relate the same of St. Bartholomew the Apostle.

The good thief received the forgiveness of his sins, but, before asking it, he humbled himself, avowing before the whole world what he was, and what he had deserved. "We receive the due reward of our deeds." (*Luke* 23:41). The woman of Canaan suffers herself to be compared to a dog by Our Lord Jesus Christ; she does not feel herself insulted by this comparison, believing, as she did, that she deserved this name. Our dear Saviour wondered at this, saying: "O, woman, great is thy faith." (*Matt.* 15:28). Her faith was so great, because her humility was so profound. Hence she heard, from the mouth of Our Lord, these consoling words: "Be it done to thee as thou wilt." The Prodigal Son says: "Father, I have sinned against heaven and before thee; I am not now worthy to be called thy son; make me as one of thy hired servants." (*Luke* 15:18). The father, seeing this great humility and sorrow in his son, pardoned him, and even received him as one of his best children.

God will treat us in the same manner, if we present ourselves before Him with the same sentiments of humility and unworthiness. When Our Lord Jesus Christ said to the centurion: "I will come and heal thy servant," the centurion answered: "Lord, I am not worthy that thou shouldst enter under my roof." (*Matt.* 8:8). This humility and faith of the centurion pleased our Saviour so much that He said to him: "Go, and as thou hast believed, so be it done to thee; and the servant was healed at the same hour." (*Matt.* 8:13).

And in what manner did Our Lord Jesus Christ Himself pray? "Kneeling down, he prayed." (*Luke* 22:47). Nay, He did more: "He fell upon his face, praying and saying: my Father, if it be possible, let this chalice pass from me." (*Matt.* 26:39). St. Thais, after her conversion from her sinful life, did not even dare so much as pronounce the name of God when praying. She used to say: "Thou Who madest me, have pity on me." St. Paul the Hermit was so much accustomed to pray on his knees, and with his hands lifted up to Heaven, that he died in this posture. Is it, then, astonishing that the saints have received so many and such great favors from God, since their humility was so great, and so pleasing to Him? "To the humble God giveth grace," says the Apostle St. James. "Their prayer shall pierce the clouds." (*Ecclus.* 35:21).

"Yes," says St. Alphonsus, "should a soul have committed ever so many sins, yet the Lord will not reject it if she knows how to humble herself." "A contrite and humble heart, O God, thou wilt not despise." (*Ps.* 50:19). As He is severe and inexorable to the proud, so is He bountiful, merciful, and liberal to the humble. "Know, My daughter," said Jesus Christ one day to St. Catherine of Siena, "that whosoever shall humbly persevere in asking graces of Me, shall obtain all virtues." "Never did I," said St. Teresa, "receive more favors from the Lord, than when I humbled myself before His Divine Majesty."

III. Our Prayer Must be Fervent.

Well hath Isaias prophesied of you, saying: "This people honoreth me with their lips: but their heart is far from me." (*Matt.* 15:8). In these words our Saviour gives us to understand that a prayer which proceeds not from the heart, or which is not devout and fervent, is not heard by His Heavenly Father. There are many Christians who recite their prayers without thinking of what they say. Should they be required to tell what they asked of Our Lord, they would be at a loss for an answer. The prayers of such Christians are quite powerless with God. One "Our Father" said with fervor is better, and obtains more from God, than the entire Rosary recited a dozen times in a careless manner.

St. Bernard once saw how an angel of the Lord wrote down in a book the divine praises of each of his brethren, when they were reciting the Divine Office; some were written in letters of gold, to express the devotion and fervor with which they were recited; others in letters of silver, on account of the pure intention with which they were performed; others were written with ink, to signify that they were said by way of routine, and in a slothful manner; others, again, were written with watercolor, to indicate that they had been performed with great lukewarmness, and without devotion or fervor.

The Divine praises of some of St. Bernard's brethren were not written down at all; but instead of the chanted psalms, the following words were written: "This people honoreth me with their lips, but their heart is far from me" (*Is.* 29:13) to signify that the angel of the Lord was much displeased with this kind of prayer.

Holy angels! Show us once your book, that we may see in what colors the prayers of so many Christians are written down, especially in time of prosperity, when no calamity forces them to have recourse to God. There is good reason to fear that the prayers of many are written down in letters of ink, others in watercolor, and the greater number of them, I fear, are not written down at all; so that the devil himself must rejoice and laugh at them, as he did at the prayers of two Christians, of whom Jourdanus speaks: "They recited their prayers in so careless a manner, that, at the conclusion of it, the devil appeared, and cast an intolerable odor around, at the same time exclaiming, with great laughter: 'Such incense is due to such prayer!'"

Moreover, how many are there not who say their prayers without being at all in earnest to obtain what they ask? They recite, for instance, the "Our Father" a hundred, yea, a thousand times, without wishing at all that any of its seven petitions should be granted. Let us examine them briefly. The first petition is: "Hallowed be Thy name"; that is, "Give me, and to all men, the grace to know Thee always better and better; to honor, praise, glorify and love Thee; to comprehend the greatness of Thy blessings, the duration of Thy promises, the sublimity of Thy majesty, and the depth of Thy judgments." These are the graces which we ask in the first petition of the "Our Father." But who are those that earnestly ask for these graces, either for themselves or for others? Certainly these blessings are not asked for by any of those who, when entering the church, do not even think of bending the knee to express their faith in the name of God.

Nor are these graces asked for by those who do not desire to listen to the Divine Word in sermons and Christian instructions, that they may better learn their duty toward God, themselves, and their fellow men.

Nor are these graces asked for by those who never think of praying fervently for the conversion of sinners, heretics, Jews, or heathens; nor by those who dishonor the name of God by cursing and swearing, thus teaching others the language of the devil; nor by those who are ashamed of giving good example, who think, speak, and act badly, when others do the same; nor by all those who grievously transgress any of the commandments of God, and thus dishonor, despise, and insult the name of God. All such men certainly do not praise and honor God's name, and yet with their lips they will always pray, "Hallowed be Thy name," without contributing anything at all toward the glory of the Lord of Heaven and earth. Of these we must think that they know not what they ask, or do not wish to obtain what they ask.

The second petition is, "Thy kingdom come." Where are those who truly wish that God alone should reign in their hearts, and that no creature should have any part in it? Alas! Most men feel provoked at the least temporal loss, at the slightest harsh word. And what account do the generality of men make of the grace and friendship of God? The readiness with which they commit sin tells it sufficiently. How difficult is it not for the priest to prevail upon them so far as to make them go to confession and Holy Communion? How seldom do they pray? Shall we then believe that those who neglect and refuse the means to acquire the grace of God are in earnest, when they pray "Thy kingdom come"?

And where are those who truly desire to leave this world for a better one? Alas! Should death knock at their door, what mourning, what alarm, what tears would it produce. Nay, many even are so much attached to this life, that, should God offer them the choice between Heaven and earth, they would prefer the latter. Let them pray, sigh, and exclaim, "Thy kingdom come," their prayer is not true, because they do not wish for God's kingdom.

And where are those who are in earnest when they pray: "Thy will be done on earth, as it is in Heaven"? Were God to say to them: "Well, it is My will that you should undergo humiliations and contempt on the part of your neighbor, of your friend, of your companion. Like Job, you shall lose your good name, your honor among your fellow men, or your children, and all your earthly goods"; how soon would every one of them change his prayer, and say: "Lord, be it otherwise done to me, as I do not mean this when I pray: 'Thy will be done on earth, as it is in Heaven.'"

The fourth petition is: "Give us this day our daily bread"; that is, give us everything necessary for the support of our temporal and spiritual life. Of course, no one refuses the temporal; but where are those who truly hunger and thirst after the food of their souls, after prayer, the word of God, confession and Holy Communion? As this food is relished but by the smallest number of men, it is evident that the greater part of them do not wish to be heard when they make this petition.

"And forgive us our trespasses, as we forgive them that have trespassed against us." Neither does this fifth petition of the "Our Father" proceed from the heart of most men. They all, of course, wish that God should forgive them every sin, guilt and punishment, but they themselves do not like to forgive. How long do they not harbor in their hearts a certain aversion, rancor, even enmity, against those of their fellow men who offended them by a little harsh word? To salute them, to speak to or pray for them, seems too hard. How can they be sincere in saying: "Forgive us our trespasses, as we forgive them that have trespassed against us"? As they ask forgiveness of God in the same way as they forgive others, they cannot be in earnest when they pray for forgiveness; their prayer is untrue; otherwise, they would forgive their fellow men.

"Lead us not into temptation"; that is, Lord, preserve us from the temptations of the devil, of the flesh, and of the world. But, alas! Most men love the occasion of temptations, and betake themselves wilfully unto it. How should the Lord, then, preserve them from temptations? Most assuredly they do not wish at all to be heard in making this petition.

"And deliver us from evil"; that is, preserve us from sin; but the greater number of men commit sins deliberately every day, not doing the least violence to themselves by trying to avoid the occasions of sin, or to have recourse to prayer in the moment of temptation, or to receive the sacraments frequently. As they do not make use of the means which God has given us to be preserved from sin, how can they pray in truth or in earnest: "Deliver us from evil"? They do not mean it.

Such a prayer is worthless in the eyes of the Lord; He will never hear us, unless we are in earnest to obtain what we pray for. "Wilt thou be made whole?" (*John* 5:6) said Our Lord to the man languishing thirty-eight years. "What will ye that I do to you?" (*Matt.* 2:32) Our Lord asked the two blind men. Had He noticed that they were not in earnest in their petition for health, He would have left them alone. Holy Scripture says of those who pray to God in earnest and with fervor, that they *cry* to the Lord. Thus holy David says of himself: "In my trouble I *cried* to the Lord, and he heard me." (*Ps.* 119:1). And the Lord has promised to hear such a prayer. "He shall *cry* to me, and I will hear him." (*Ps.* 90:15). Now to cry to the Lord means, according to St. Bernard, to pray with a great desire to be heard. The greater this desire is, the more piercing is this cry of prayer to the ears of God.

In vain do we hope that God will hear our prayer, if it be destitute of this earnest desire, fervor, sighing, crying, and effusion of the heart. Hence the prophet Jeremias says: "Arise, give praise in the night, in the beginning of the watches; pour out thy heart like water before the face of the Lord; lift up thy hands to him for the life of thy little children that have fainted for hunger." (*Lam.* 2:19). Now what is it to pour out our heart before the Lord? It is to pray, to sigh, to cry with a most vehement desire to be heard by Our Lord. Hence St. Bernard says: "A vehement desire is great crying in the ears of the Lord," for God considers more the ardent desire and love of the heart than the cries of the lips. And St. Paul says in his Epistle to the Romans: "The Spirit himself asketh for us with *unspeakable groanings.*" (*Rom.* 8:26). Hence the royal prophet says of his prayer: "In his sight I pour out my prayer." (*Ps.* 14:3). And in *Ps.* 61:9 he says: *"Pour out your heart* before him." It was thus that Anna poured out her heart before the Lord, and obtained the holy child Samuel. "As Anna had her heart full of grief, she prayed to the Lord, shedding many tears; and it came to pass, as she multiplied prayers before the Lord," etc. (*1 Kgs.* 1:10, 12).

Here the holy Fathers ask what is meant by this long prayer of Anna, since she besought the Lord only in a few words to grant her a child. St. John Chrysostom answers, and says: "Although her prayer consisted of but few words, yet it was long, on account of the interior fervor and ardent desire with which she poured out her heart before the Lord, for she prayed more with her heart than with her lips, according to what is related in Holy Scripture: 'Now Anna spoke from her heart, whilst her lips only moved, but her voice was silent.'" (*1 Kings* 1:13). Our Lord will, therefore, hear us, provided we understand how to pour out our hearts in prayer—that is, to lay open before Him all the wishes and desires of our soul, its griefs, sufferings, cares, solicitudes, and anxieties, laying them, as it were, into His paternal heart, and into the bosom of His Divine providence, in order that He may come to aid, relieve and comfort us.

Nay, according to St. Paul, we ought to do still more. In his Epistle to the Ephesians we read: "By all prayer and supplication, praying at all times in the spirit." (*Eph.* 6:18). In these words the Apostle gives us to understand that we should pray so earnestly and fervently to God, as to sigh, cry, strike our breast, falling prostrate on the ground; nay, even conjure the Lord, by the death and Blood of Jesus Christ, and by everything sacred, thus to move Him to grant our prayer. Should we experience, in our will, a certain languor, sloth and tepidity, nay, even a certain repugnance and resistance to ask favors of God with fervor and earnestness, we must beseech our dear Lord, as the Holy Church does in one of her prayers, to compel our rebellious wills, by means best calculated to enkindle this holy fervor in our hearts, in order that we may make sure of being heard, and of receiving what we pray for.

In order to produce this holy fervor in our hearts, God often sends us troubles, crosses, sickness, and adversities of every description, nothing being better calculated to make us pray with fervor than afflictions, tribulations and crosses. Let the soul be under heavy sufferings, which it would like to cast off, surely it will not need a prayerbook. It is then that, like hungry beggars, it finds a flow of words to produce the most heartfelt and fervent prayer. In prosperous times the prayerbook is recurred to, but in the hour of adversity it is the heart that speaks, from an over-great desire to be relieved and comforted. It is then that men say, with David: "All the day I cried to thee, O Lord! I stretched out my hands to thee." (*Ps.* 87:10). "Consider and hear me, O Lord, my God!" (*Ps.* 12:4). Such prayers are most pleasing to God, and He cannot help hearing them, according to what David says: "In my trouble I cried to the Lord, and he heard me." (*Ps.* 119:1).

When the Prophet Jonas was swallowed by the whale and carried about in the depths of the ocean, he prayed most fervently to the Lord his God, saying: "Thou hast cast me forth into the heart of the deep sea, and a flood hath encompassed me; all thy billows and waves have passed over me." (*Jon.* 2:4). He then said: "I cried out of my affliction to the Lord, and *he heard me.* I cried out of the belly of hell, and *thou hast heard my voice." (Jon.* 3). How great was the affliction of Sara, on being accused of having murdered seven husbands, who had been killed by a devil named Asmodeus, at their first going in unto her. At this reproach, says Holy Scripture, she went into an upper chamber of her house, and for three days and three nights did neither eat nor drink, but, continuing in prayer with tears, besought God to deliver her from this reproach. "And her prayers were heard, in the sight of the glory of the Most High God." (*Job* 3:24). With what fervor did not the Apostles cry out to Our Lord Jesus Christ, amidst the storms of the sea: "Lord save us, we perish"? And He heard their cry, and commanded the winds and the sea, and there came a great calm. (*Matt.* 8:25-26). Yes, in tribulation is truly verified what is related of the ruler in the Gospel: "And he himself believed, and his whole house." (*John* 4:53). It is, then, that not only one member of the family will pray; nay, father, mother, children, servants, relatives, will unite in beseeching the Lord for assistance, because grief and affliction have come upon the whole house. Thus the Latin proverb is verified: *"Qui nescit orare, eat ad mare."* Let him who does not know how to pray with fervor, make a voyage at sea. There the storms and dangers of death will teach him to pour forth most fervent prayers. Such prayers are most powerful with, and they are heard by, the Lord.

I cannot omit remarking that tears shed during prayer are most powerful with God to obtain our petitions. The Fathers of the Church are profuse in bestowing praises upon humble tears of the soul. The Holy Scriptures and the lives of the saints abound in examples to prove their power with God. "Oh, how great is the power which the tears of sinners exercise with God!" exclaims St. Peter Chrysologus. (*Serm.* 93). "They water Heaven, wash the earth clean, deliver from Hell, and prevail upon God to recall the sentence of damnation pronounced over every mortal sin." "Yes," says Anselmus Laudunensis, commenting on the words of the Book of Tobias, " 'continuing in prayer, with tears he besought God.' (*Tob.* 3:11). Prayer appeases God, but, if tears are added, He feels overcome, and unable to resist any longer. The former is for him an odoriferous balm, the latter is a sweet tyranny."

Hence Julianus (*Lib. de Ligno Vitae,* chap. 9) exclaims, with truth: "O humble tears, how great is your power, how great is your reign! You need not fear the Tribunal of the Eternal Judge; you silence all your accusers, and no one dares prevent you from approaching the Lord; should you enter alone, you will not come out empty. Moreover, you conquer the unconquerable, you bind the Omnipotent, you open Heaven, you chase all the devils."

"Indeed," says Peter Cellensis (*Lib. de Panibus,* chap. 12), "the infernal spirits find the flames of Hell more supportable than our tears." Cornelius à Lapide says: "One tear of the sinner, produced by the sorrow of his heart, is capable of making God forgive and forget many, even the most atrocious crimes." For this reason St. Leo, the Pope, says of the tears of St. Peter, "O happy tears of thine, O holy Apostle St. Peter, which were for thee a holy baptism to cancel thy sin of denying the Lord." (*Serm. 9, de Passione*). St. Magdalen asks of Our Lord the forgiveness of her numerous and great sins; but in what manner? "She began to wash his sacred feet with her tears" (*Luke* 7:38); these tears moved His compassionate heart, and made Him say, "Many sins are forgiven her, because she hath loved much."

Why was it that the holy patriarch Jacob, when wrestling with the angel of the Lord, received His blessing? (*Gen.* 32). It was because he asked it with tears in his eyes: "He *wept,* and made supplication to him." (*Osee* 12:4). In the Fourth Book of Kings, we read as follows: "In these days Ezechias was sick unto death, and Isaias the Prophet came to him and said: Thus saith the Lord God: Give charge concerning thy house, for thou shalt die, and not live. And he turned his face to the wall, and prayed to the Lord, saying: I beseech thee, O Lord, remember how I have walked before thee in truth, and with a perfect heart, and have done that which is pleasing before thee. And Ezechias *wept with much weeping."* (*4 Kgs.* 20:1-3). What did he obtain by his tears? Holy Writ says: "And before Isaias was gone out of the middle of the court, the word of the Lord came to him, saying: Go back and tell Ezechias: thus saith the Lord: I have heard thy prayer and I have seen thy *tears;* and behold I have healed thee; on the third day thou shalt go up to the Temple of the Lord. And I will add to thy days fifteen years."

Our Lord Jesus Christ Himself often prayed with tears in His eyes, according to what St. Paul the Apostle writes: "Who, in the days of his flesh, *with a strong cry and tears, offering up prayers and supplication, was heard* for his reverence." (*Heb.* 5:7). In his comment on Zacharias, Cornelius à Lapide relates that St. Dunstan, after the death of King Edwin, from whom he had received much ill-treatment, saw whilst at prayer several black men running off with the soul of the king in their hands. (*Zach.* 12). Forgetting all the injuries and ill-treatment which he had received from Edwin, he took pity on him in his miserable condition, shedding *torrents of tears* before the face of the Lord, for the deliverance of the king's soul, and he did not cease weeping and praying until the Lord heard him. Soon after he saw the same black men again, but their hands were empty, and the soul of the king was no longer in their possession. They then commenced to curse and swear, and utter the most abominable imprecations against the servant of God, to which St. Dunstan paid no attention, but thanked God for the extraordinary great mercy shown to the king.

Let us, then, with Judith (*Jdt.* 8:14), pray to the Lord, and ask with tears His pardon, His graces, and all His favors; and let us rest assured, that as a mother cannot help consoling her weeping child, neither will our dear Lord refuse to hear the petitions of weeping souls.

IV. *Our Prayer must be followed by Amendment of Life.*

The sinner who prays to God for salvation without having the desire to quit the state of sin must not expect to be heard. "There are," says St. Alphonsus, "some unhappy persons who love the chains with which the devil keeps them bound like slaves. The prayers of such are never heard by God, because they are rash, presumptuous, and abominable." The prayer of him who turns away his ears so as not to hear what God commands, is detestable and odious to God: "He who turneth away his ears from hearing the law, his prayer shall be an abomination." (*Prov.* 28:9). To these people God says: "It is of no use your praying to me, for I will turn my eyes from you, and will not hear you; when you stretch forth your hands I will turn away my eyes from you, and when you multiply prayer I will not hear." (*Is.* 1:15).

Why was the Lord so severe to the Jews, His chosen people, inflicting upon them the hardest punishments, such as the Egyptian bondage, in which they suffered for so many years? How often did they not pray for their deliverance? And why did the Lord not hear them? The prophet Ezechiel says: "And they committed fornication in Egypt; in their youth they committed fornication." (*Ezech.* 23:8). Hence they prayed and cried to God in vain. But no sooner had they done away with their sins of idolatry and fornication, than the Lord graciously heard them: "And the children of Israel, groaning, cried out because of the works; and their cry went up unto God from the works, and he heard their groaning, and remembered the covenant which he had made with Abraham, Isaac, and Jacob; and the Lord looked upon the children of Israel, and he knew them." (*Ex.* 2:23-25).

The Ark of the Covenant was a great treasure for the Jews. When it was carried around the city of Jericho, the walls of the city fell down; when the Jews had arrived with it at the River Jordan, the waters of the river divided, the lower part flowing off, and the upper part rising like a mountain. Now after the Jews had lost four thousand men in one day, in a war against the Philistines, they had the Ark brought into the camp, hoping that, for its sake, the Lord would protect them, and deliver their enemies into their hands. And the ancients of Israel said: "Why hath the Lord defeated us today before the Philistines? Let us fetch unto us the ark of the covenant of the Lord from Silo, and let it come in the midst of us, that it may save us from the hands of our enemies. And when the ark of the covenant of the Lord was come into the camp, all Israel shouted with a great joy, and the earth rang again." (*1 Kings* 4:3, 5). Now they thought they had no more to fear from their enemies, who, at the sight of the Ark of the Covenant, were panic-stricken; so much so, that they cried out, "God is come into the camp." And sighing they said, "Woe to us; who shall deliver us from the hands of these high gods?" (*1 Kgs.* 4:7-8).

With new courage the Jews began to fight again. Were they victorious? By no means; they were defeated worse than ever, losing thirty thousand men, besides the Ark of the Covenant. One might ask here: Did God then cease to love the Israelites? Most assuredly not. His love still remained the same as before. Why, then, were they defeated in the presence of the Ark of the Covenant, which was given to them as a sign of the Divine blessing and protection? "But for the love of His Ark," says Theodoret, "God did not wish to protect His people, because, after having previously offended Him, they did not repent of their sins. It was with sinful hearts they paid outward honor to the Ark. They shouted with great joy as soon as they beheld it, but there was not one who shed a tear of repentance, no one prayed and sighed with a sorrowful heart. Hence the Ark brought down no blessing upon them at that time."

"Why, then, should we wonder," says Dionysius the Carthusian, "if we see miseries and calamities increase among the Christians, notwithstanding their prayer to avert them. 'Tis because they pray with sinful and criminal hearts, not being sorry in the least for their evil deeds, nor showing the slightest desire to amend their lives." Let them wear upon their person as many *Agnus Deis,* relics of the saints, Gospels of St. John, as they may wish; let them pray, nay, even cry to Heaven as much as they will, all these articles of devotion, prayers, and cries will avail them nothing, if, at the same time, they are given up to the devil, and do not wish to give up his worship and service. Instead of being heard, they will, according to St. Augustine, be so much the more severely punished. "Punishments," says the saint, "become more frequent every day, because the number of sins is daily increasing."

If we, then, wish that God should hear our prayers, we must be sorry for our sins, and endeavor to amend our lives. "Above all," says St. Ambrose, "we must weep, and then pray." The Lord Himself has declared this quite distinctly by the Prophet Isaias: "I will not hear you"—why not? "For your hands are full of blood" (*Is.* 1:15); full of sins and iniquities.

But on the contrary, the Lord has promised by the same prophet that He will hear the prayers of those who truly amend their lives: "Loose the bands of wickedness; undo the bundles that oppress . . . Then shalt thou call, and the Lord shall hear; thou shalt cry, and he shall say: Here I am" (*Is.* 58:6, 9)—that is, to help you. God commanded the Prophet Jonas to announce to the Ninevites that within forty days their city would be destroyed. The Ninevites at once began to pray to God, and ask His pardon. God heard their prayers. Why? Because they repented of their sins, did penance for them, and amended their lives.

The prayers of a true and sincere penitent are acceptable in the sight of God, and are heard by Him. Hence, according to the advice of St. Paul, we must endeavor always to pray to God with a contrite heart. "I will, therefore," says this Apostle, "that men pray in every place, lifting up pure hands." (*1 Tim.* 2:8). When are our hearts pure? "When they are free from sin," says St. Ambrose.

From what has been said, the sinner should, however, not infer that as he is a sinner, and in disgrace with God, his prayer could not be acceptable to God, and that therefore he should cease praying. No, it would be entirely wrong for a sinner to argue thus; for as long as he does not sin unto death, that is, if he has not the will to live and die in sin, but desires to amend his life, and prays for this grace, God will listen to his prayer, and hear it, if he perseveres in his petition. "There are others," says St. Alphonsus, "who sin through frailty, or by the violence of some great passion, who groan under the yoke of the enemy, and desire to break these chains of death, and to escape from their miserable slavery. Let such ask the assistance of God; for their prayer, if persevered in, will certainly be heard, Jesus Christ having said: 'Every one that asketh, receiveth, and he who seeketh, findeth.'" (*Matt.* 7:8).

His prayer, it is true, is not heard on account of his meritorious works, which he does not possess, but it is heard on account of the merits of Jesus Christ, and because our Saviour has promised to hear everyone who asks. "Therefore, when we pray," says St. Thomas, "it is not necessary to be friends of God in order to obtain the grace we ask; for prayer itself restores us to His friendship." Hence St. Bernard says: "The desire of the sinner to escape from sin is a gift which is certainly given by no other than God Himself, who most undoubtedly would not give this holy desire to the sinner, unless He intended to hear him." Witness the publican in the Gospel, who went into the temple to pray: "And the publican standing afar off, would not so much as lift up his eyes towards heaven, but struck his breast, saying: O God, be merciful to me a sinner! I say to you, this man went down into his house justified." (*Luke* 18:13-14).

But the sinner may say I have no sorrow for my sins, and I do not desire to amend my life; therefore, according to what you have said, God will not hear my prayer, consequently I may abandon it altogether. I answer, by no means give up your prayer, although God will not hear you so long as you persevere in these dispositions of heart; yet for the sake of your prayer, God spares you, waiting patiently for your conversion. "No sinner," says St. Alphonsus, "should ever give up his prayer, as otherwise he would be lost forever. God would send sinners to Hell sooner if they ceased praying, yet, on account of their perseverance in prayer, He still spares them."

But let him who has no sorrow for his sins, no desire for the amendment of his life, let him ask of God this sorrow and grace of a thorough conversion, and let him persevere in asking for it. If he does, he may rest assured that God will finally enlighten his mind by making him understand the miserable state in which he is living, and touch his heart with sorrow for it; besides, God will also strengthen the will of the sinner, so as to be able to make serious efforts to rise from this fatal state.

Another will say, I have not only no sorrow for my sins, but I have not even the least desire to ask God's grace to be sorry for them. How can I, then, pray, not having the least desire to obtain anything? This, I must confess, is a pitiable, but not a desperate, state; for, if you will pray with perseverance, God will give you the desire to pray for the grace of contrition. Has He not declared: "I desire not the death of the wicked, but that he be converted and live"? God has the greatest desire to see all sinners saved, and He is ready at any time to give them the graces necessary for their salvation; but He wishes that they should pray for every good thought and desire, and for efficacious grace to put their good desires into execution. Let such a sinner pray: "Lord, give me a true desire to pray to Thee for my salvation"; let him persevere in thus praying, and then let him rest assured that he will not be lost.

The conversion of King Manasses is a most striking proof of this truth. Manasses was twelve years old when his father died. He succeeded him on the throne, but not in his piety and fear of the Lord. He was as impious as his father was pious toward God and His people. He introduced again all the abominations of the Gentiles, which the Lord had extirpated from among the children of Israel; he apostatized from the Lord; he brought in again, and encouraged, idolatry; even in the Temple of the Lord he erected an altar to Baal; he introduced into the Temple of the true God such abominations as were never heard of before, and which are too shameful to relate. To crown his impiety, he made his son pass through fire in honor of Moloch; he used divination, observed omens, appointed pythons, and multiplied soothsayers, to do evil before the Lord, and to provoke Him. (*4 Kings* 21:1-7). The Lord often warned him through His prophets, but in vain. At last "The Lord spoke to His prophets, saying: Because

Manasses, king of Juda, hath done these most wicked abominations, beyond all that the Amorrhites did before him, and hath made Juda also to sin with his filthy doings, therefore, thus saith the Lord the God of Israel: Behold, I will bring evils upon Jerusalem and Juda, that whosoever shall hear of them, both his ears shall tingle. I will stretch over Jerusalem the line of Samaria and the weight of the house of Achab, and I will efface Jerusalem, as tables are wont to be effaced . . . and I will deliver them into the hands of their enemies, and they shall become a prey and a spoil to all their enemies." (*4 Kings* 21:10-14).

Manasses, instead of entering into himself, added cruelty to idolatry. He shed so much innocent blood, that, to use the words of Holy Writ, "He filled Jerusalem up to the mouth." (*4 Kings* 21:16). According to Josephus, "He went so far in his contempt for God as to kill all the just of the children of Israel, not sparing even the prophets, but taking away their lives day by day, so that streams of blood were flowing through the streets of Jerusalem." (*Ant.* 10:13). Now do you think so impious a wretch could be converted? Oh, wonderful power of prayer! So great is thy efficacy with God, that should a man be ever so impious and perverse, he will not fail to obtain forgiveness of the Lord, if he pray for it with a sincere heart. "And the Lord," says Holy Writ, "brought upon Jerusalem the captains of the army of the king of the Assyrians, and they took Manasses and carried him, bound with chains and fetters, to Babylon. In this great distress and affliction he entered into himself, and he prayed to the Lord his God, and did penance exceedingly before the God of his fathers, and he entreated him, and he besought him earnestly; and the Lord heard his prayer, and brought him again to Jerusalem into his kingdom. From that time forward he endeavored to serve the Lord the more fervently, the more grievously he had offended Him. He abolished idolatry, destroyed the temples, altars, groves on the high places, put up in honor of heathenish deities; repaired the altar of Jehovah, in the temple of Jerusalem, and sacrificed upon it victims and peace offerings, and offerings of praise, and he commanded Juda to serve the Lord the God of Israel." (*2 Par.* 33:10-16).

I again repeat what I have said elsewhere: How great will be the pain and misery of the damned, seeing that they might have been saved so easily, provided they had prayed to God for their salvation. How true is not what St. Alphonsus says: "All spiritual writers in their books, all preachers in their sermons, all confessors in their instructions to their penitents, should not inculcate anything more strongly than continual prayer, they should always admonish, exclaim, and continually repeat: Pray, pray, never cease to pray, for if you pray, your salvation will be secure; but if you leave off praying, your damnation will be certain. All preachers and directors ought to do this, because, according to the opinion of every Catholic school, there is no doubt of this truth, that he who prays obtains grace, and is saved; but those who practice it are too few, and this is why so few are saved." (Chap. 4, on Prayer).

V. Our Prayer must be United with Forgiveness of Injuries.

"And when you shall stand to pray, forgive, if you have aught against any man." (*Mark* 11:25). "Leave thy offering before the altar, and go first to be reconciled to thy brother, and then coming, thou shalt offer thy gift " (*Matt.* 5:24).

In these words, Our Lord Jesus Christ teaches us that our prayer will not be heard by His heavenly Father so long as we entertain in our hearts feelings of dislike toward any of our fellow men. If you have recourse to prayer, He says, and at the same time have aught against any man, go first, and be reconciled to your brother, or at least forgive him from the bottom of your heart, and then come and offer up your prayers; otherwise I will not listen to you. He has made every man his representative on earth, by creating him according to His own image and likeness; He has redeemed all men with His most precious Blood; He has therefore declared that whatever we do to the least of our fellow men for His sake, we do it to Him. Now, by commanding us to love our enemies, to do good to those that hate us, and to pray for those that persecute and calumniate us (*Matt.* 5:44), He asks of us to give to Him in the person of His representatives that which we can give so easily. It would be great presumption to ask His gifts and favors, without being willing, on our part, to give Him what He requires of us in all justice. To refuse this request of Our Lord would, indeed, on our part, be great injustice. We ask of Him the greatest gifts, such as the pardon of innumerable and most grievous offenses, final perseverance, deliverance from Hell, everlasting glory, and so many other countless favors for both body and soul. What He asks of us is little or nothing, compared with His graces.

I will give you what I can, says He, if you give Me what you can; if you will not, neither am I bound to give anything to you. Hence I have said: "If two of you shall consent upon earth concerning anything whatsoever they shall ask, it shall be done to them by my Father who is in heaven." (*Matt.* 18:19). Our Saviour means here to say that our heavenly Father is so much pleased with the prayers of those who have no feelings of hatred toward one another, that He will grant to them whatsoever they ask of Him; but if, on the contrary, they entertain such feelings, their prayer will not be heard. "As singing is not pleasing or attractive to anyone if the voices are not in perfect harmony, so neither," says Origen, "will the prayers of Christian congregations give any pleasure to God, if they be not of one heart and one soul, nor will He hear their petitions."

We must, then, whenever we betake ourselves to prayer, banish from our hearts all willful enmity, hatred, rancor, and all uncharitable sentiments which may arise in our soul, by saying a short, but fervent prayer for all those toward whom such feelings arise, or by offering up to God for each one of them the precious Blood of Jesus Christ, and all His merits, in union with those of His Blessed Mother, and of all His saints.

To pray for those who wish us evil is an extremely difficult act, and one of the most heroic charity. It is an act free of self-love and self-interest, which is not only counselled, but even commanded by Our Lord. (*Matt.* 5:44). The insults, calumnies, and persecutions of our enemies relate directly to our own person; wherefore, if we forgive, nay, even beg God also to forgive our enemies, we give up our claim to our right and honor, thus raising ourselves to the great dignity of true children of God, nay, even to an unspeakably sublime resemblance to His Divinity, according to what Jesus Christ says: "If you pray for those who hate, calumniate and persecute you, you will be children of your Father who is in heaven, who maketh his sun to rise upon the good and bad, and raineth upon the just and the unjust." (*Matt.* 5:45). For with God nothing is more characteristic, nothing more honorable, than to have mercy and to spare; to do good to all His enemies, thus converting them to become His friends, His children, and heirs of His everlasting glory.

Now, by imitating His goodness in a point most averse to our nature, we give Him the greatest glory; and do such violence to His tender and meek Heart as to cause It not only to forgive the sin of our enemies, but even to constrain it to grant all our prayers; because He wishes to be far more indulgent, far more merciful, and far more liberal than it is possible for us ever to be. Holy Scripture, and the lives of the saints, furnish us with most striking examples in proof of this great and most consoling truth.

The greatest persecutor of St. Stephen was St. Paul the Apostle, before his conversion; for, according to St. Augustine, he threw stones at him by the hands of all those whose clothes he was guarding. What made him, from being a persecutor of the Church, become her greatest Apostle and Doctor? It was the prayer of St. Stephen; "For, had he not prayed," says St. Augustine, "the Church would not have gained this Apostle." St. Mary Oigni, whilst in a rapture, saw how Our Lord presented St. Stephen with the soul of St. Paul, before his death, on account of the prayer which the former had offered for him; she saw how St. Stephen received the soul of this Apostle, the moment of his death, and how he presented it to Our Lord, saying: "Here, O Lord, I have the immense and most precious gift which Thou gavest me; now I return it to Thee with great usury." (*Her Life,* by Cardinal Vitriaco, lib. 2, chap. 11). (Ecomen is of opinion that, on account of St. Stephen's prayer, not only St. Paul, but many others most probably received the forgiveness of their sins and life everlasting.).

In many instances St. Stephen has proved to be a most powerful intercessor and patron of all those who wish to convert, not only their enemies, but also other obstinate sinners. God granted him this power for his zeal, his example, and his martyrdom. Let us often invoke him to pray for our enemies, as he did for his.

Most touching is that which Father Avila relates of St. Elizabeth of Hungary: One day this saint prayed to God to give great graces to all those who had in any way injured her; nay, even to give the greatest graces to those who had injured her the most. After this prayer, Our Lord Jesus

Christ said to her: "My dear daughter, never in your life did you make a prayer more pleasing to Me than the one which you have just said for your enemies; on account of this prayer, I forgive not only all your sins, but even all temporal punishments due to them." Let us be sure that the greater injuries we forgive for God's sake, the greater graces we shall receive in answer to our prayer.

We read, in the life of St. John Gualbertus, that he met one day with the murderer of his only brother, in a very narrow street. Fearing that John would take revenge on him, and seeing no possibility of escape, the murderer fell on his knees, asking forgiveness for the sake of Our Lord Jesus Christ, who forgave His murderers, and prayed for them on the Cross. John forgave him at once, and embraced him as one of his best friends. Afterwards he went to a church, there to pray before a crucifix; but oh, how pleasing was his prayer now to Our Lord, and how powerful was it with Him! Whilst praying, he saw how Our Lord bowed His head toward him, thanking him, as it were, for the great offense he had forgiven. At the same time he felt a most extraordinary change in his own soul, to such a degree that he renounced the world, and became the founder of a religious Order.

But some might say: I have no enemies; hence I have nothing to forgive, and thus I cannot use this means to make my prayer efficacious. In this case, say to God: Had I, O Lord, a thousand enemies, for Thy sake I would forgive, love, and pray for them. Thus you will practice, at least in desire, the highest degree of charity, and Our Lord will take the will for the deed. But you must remember that, if you have no opportunity to practice this degree of charity in reality, you will always find plenty of occasions to practice the degree next to it; which consists in bearing with your neighbors' whims, weaknesses, faults of character, disagreeable manners, and the like, trying to make yourself all to all. The practice of this kind of charity will equally move Our Lord graciously to listen to your prayers.

In proof of this, we have but to consider the example of Moses. Notwithstanding the frequent murmurs of the Jewish people, their reproaches, their rebellion, their apostasy, he acted toward them with the same unvarying kindness; instead of taking revenge, he poured forth fervent prayers to God for their temporal and spiritual welfare. Hence it was that his prayer was so powerful with God as to prevent Him from punishing the Jews for their sins, so long as Moses interceded and asked Him to pardon them. On this account, St. Jerome, St. Thomas, Hugo, Theodoret, and others, say that when this meek and forbearing charity is praying, it forces God, as it were, to listen to and hear its prayer. Let this be remembered by those especially who guide and direct others.

VI. Our Prayer must be united with Good Works.

"And thy justice shall go before thy face." (*Is.* 58:8). St. Cyprian, commenting on these words of Isaias, says: "God will listen to and hear those prayers which are joined to good works." The angel of the Lord said to Tobias: "Prayer is good with fasting and alms" (*Tob.* 12:8); and by the prophet Isaias the Lord says: "Deal thy bread to the hungry, and bring the needy and the harborless into thy house; when thou shalt see one naked, cover him, and despise not thy own flesh." (*Is.* 58:7). "Seek judgment, relieve the oppressed, judge for the fatherless, defend the widow." (*Is.* 1:17). "Then shalt thou call, and the Lord shall hear; thou shalt cry, and he shall say: Here I am." (*Is.* 58:9).

And again it is said: "Blessed are the merciful, for they shall obtain mercy" (*Matt.* 5:7); especially when they pray, for whosoever is good and liberal to the brethren of Jesus

Christ on earth, to him Jesus Christ must be good, and liberal also; for He is, and He desires to exhibit Himself infinitely better than anyone possibly could be. We read in the life of the Bishop St. Julian that he distributed among the poor and needy everything he possessed. Hence the Church says of him that, being inflamed with a great paternal charity for his fellow men, he obtained from God many wonderful things. When the people were once suffering very much from a want of corn, he began to pray to God with tears in his eyes; at once several wagons of corn arrived, and no sooner were they unloaded than the men who brought the corn disappeared. Another time, when an epidemic spread rapidly throughout the diocese of this holy bishop, God caused it suddenly to cease, on account of the prayer of His holy servant. The Lord also heard his prayer for many who suffered from incurable diseases.

But many a one may say, "It is not in my power to give alms, to fast, to wait upon the sick, or perform any such good works; hence the means just given to make prayer efficacious, is, for me, not practicable." In this case you must remember that, besides these so-called exterior good works, there are others, called interior ones, which are better calculated to make prayer very powerful with God. Of these latter I will mention but one, viz.: the denial of your own will, in order to do God's will in the most perfect manner. "If thou hear the voice of the Lord thy God" (*Deut.* 30:10), or, as Isaias says, "If thou turn away thy foot from doing thy own will" (*Is.* 58:13), in order to follow Mine, as it is expressed in My commandments, in the doctrine of My Son, and thy Redeemer, and in thy rules, if thou art a religious; in the precepts of those who keep My place with thee on earth, and in My inspirations, I also will listen to thy voice when thou prayest to Me. Hence Cornelius à Lapide says: "If you wish that God should do your will when praying, you must first do what

He wishes and commands you. If you wish that He should turn to you, you must go to meet Him; if you desire that He should delight in you, you must delight in Him." "Delight in the Lord," says the Psalmist, "and he will give thee the requests of thy heart." (*Ps.* 36:4).

Now who can be said in truth to go and meet the Lord, and delight in Him? He only who, with a cheerful heart, does the Lord's will. "His petitions," as the royal prophet says, "shall be granted." Hence Our Lord said one day to St. Gertrude, when she was praying for one of her sisters in religion, who wished that God should grant her prayer for Divine consolations: "It is she herself who puts obstacles to the consolations of My grace by the attachment to her own will and judgment. As one who closes his nostrils cannot enjoy the fragrancy of fresh flowers, so, in like manner, the sweet consolations of My grace cannot be experienced by him who is attached to his own will and judgment."

Our Lord Jesus Christ expressed this also very clearly in His last discourse to His disciples, wherein He dwells particularly upon the three most essential virtues of Faith, Hope, and Charity; of Faith, by saying, "You believe in God, believe also in me" (*John* 14:1); of Hope, by saying, in verse 13: "Whatsoever you shall ask the Father in my name, that I will do" (prayer being an act of Hope); of Charity, by saying: "If you love me, keep my commandments." (*John* 14:15). These three virtues are most intimately connected with one another; for Faith produces Hope, and Hope generates Charity. The meaning, then, is this: If you wish to obtain what I promised you, and to receive what you ask in My name; nay, if you wish that I may ask it for you of My Heavenly Father, or may even give it Myself to you, you must love Me, who have loved you so very much, and you must persevere and increase in love of Me. Now you will accomplish this by keeping My commandments. If you faithfully and perseveringly comply with this wish of Mine, I promise you an immense reward, viz., the Paraclete, the Holy Ghost: "And I will ask the Father, and he will give you another Paraclete." (*John* 14:16).

The grant of our petitions in prayer depends, then, on our faithful fulfillment of the will of God. "You ought to know, brethren, that God will comply with our wishes in prayer only in proportion as we try to comply with His commandments." (*Auct. Serm. ad Frat. in eremo, apud St. Aug. tom. 10, Serm. 61*). Hence we must not be astonished if we see or hear how the saints obtained everything from God. "He who honoreth his father, . . . in the day of his prayer he shall be heard." (*Ecclus.* 3:6). For those who honor their heavenly Father most perfectly, by an exact compliance with His Divine will, He honors by doing their will.

St. Francis of Assisi would often stop on his journey suddenly, as soon as he perceived within himself an interior inspiration of God, and giving it all his attention, he would say: "Speak, O Lord, for thy servant heareth!" He would stop as long as the inspiration lasted, listening to it in all humility, and promptly executing whatever Our Lord would inspire him to do. Hence he became so great and powerful with God. One day, as he was praying in these words, "Lord, have compassion on poor sinners," Jesus Christ appeared to him, saying: "Francis, thy will is one with Mine; I am therefore ready to grant all thy prayers."

For this reason it is that Cornelius à Lapide exclaims: "Oh, how powerful should we be with God, were we always to lend a ready ear and an obedient heart to His voice!" Like St. Dominic, we would experience that there is nothing that could not be obtained by prayer. Indeed, so good is Our Lord to those who do His will perfectly, that

He not only grants their prayers, but even anticipates them. Tauler relates of a pious virgin, whose spiritual director he was, that many people used to come and recommend their affairs to her prayers. (Serm. 1, *De Circumsis*). She always promised to pray for them, but often forgot to do so. Nevertheless, the wishes of those who had recommended themselves to her prayers were fulfilled. These persons then came and thanked her, feeling persuaded that through her prayers God had helped them. The pious virgin blushed, and confessed that although she had intended to pray for them, she had forgotten to do so. Wishing to know the reason why Our Lord blessed all those who recommended themselves to her prayers, she said to Him: "Why, O Lord, is it that Thou dost bless all those who recommend themselves to my prayers, even though I do forget to pray for them?" Our Lord answered her: "My daughter, from that very day on which you gave up your will, in order always to do Mine, I gave up Mine to do yours, wherefore I even comply with the pious intentions which you forget to carry out."

Thus is verified what the Lord promised by the prophet Isaias: "And it shall come to pass that before they call I will hear." (*Is.* 65:24). Would to God that all men would understand what has just been said, and practice it most faithfully! How happy would they make themselves, and others. Let us often say the following prayer of the Church, or one similar to it: "O Almighty and Eternal God, give us an increase in Faith, Hope, and Charity; and in order that we may deserve to obtain what Thou promisest, make us *love what Thou commandest*."

VII. Our Prayer must be Confident.

According to the Apostle St. James, one of the principal defects of prayer is a want of confidence in God that He will hear our petition. "Let him," says the Apostle, "who wavereth [that is, he who has no confidence in the Lord] not think that, when he prays, he will receive anything of Him." "A diffident prayer," says St. Bernard, "cannot penetrate into Heaven"; because immoderate fear restrains the soul so much, that, when she prays, she not only has no courage to raise herself to Heaven, but she dares not even so much as stir. Now she hopes to be heard, then she doubts, saying to herself: "I shall obtain what I ask; no, I shall not. God will grant what I pray for; no, He will not do so, or He will do so when too late. He will give it sparingly. I deserve to be heard; no, I do not deserve it. I am worthy of it; no, I am unworthy of it. God is merciful and liberal; but He is also a just God. His mercy is great, but my sins are too numerous and too great to be heard."

Hence it happens that, in this fluctuation of thoughts and doubts, a diffident soul at one time prays to God with patience, then complains of and murmurs against Him with impatience; again she is resolved to wait until God is pleased to hear her; at another time she loses courage, and feels angry because she is not heard at once. She is, as St. James says, "like the waves of the sea, which are moved and carried about by the wind," giving herself up to these thoughts and doubts, without making any serious efforts to combat them; especially so when she meets with any troubles, adversity, cross, or the like. Thus Moses began to doubt, on account of the unworthiness of the rebellious Jews, saying: "Hear ye, rebellious and incredulous, can we bring you forth water out of this rock?" (*Num.* 20:10). In punishment for his want of confidence, he had to die in the desert. And the Lord said to Moses: "Because you have not believed Me, you shall not bring this people into the land which I will give them."

St. Peter, also, when walking upon the water at the command of Jesus, and perceiving the great wind, began to doubt, and lose confidence in the word of his Master.

Our Lord reproached him for it, saying: "O thou of little faith, why didst thou doubt?" (*Matt.* 14:31). Therefore, if we wish to be heard in prayer, we must, as the Apostle says, "pray with faith." But this faith, to be good, must have three qualities: First, it must be the right faith in its true meaning, free from hesitation or doubt, as otherwise it would be infidelity or heresy; secondly, it must include confidence, or certain, firm hope, free from diffidence or despair; and thirdly, it must comprise a firm conviction of obtaining what we ask, excluding all wavering, or the fear of not obtaining what we ask.

First. The Apostle St. James requires, for prayer, the right faith in its true bearing; and not only a general faith in God's omnipotence, providence, munificence, veracity, paternal care and love for us all—that as God, He is able, and as Father, inclined to do good to us, His children; but also a particular faith; that is, that He will give us what we ask, provided it be not detrimental to us. This is the very promise of Him who is Truth itself, and who can neither deceive nor be deceived: "And all things whatsoever you shall ask in prayer, believing, you shall receive." (*Matt.* 21:22; *Mark* 11:24).

We believe with a Divine faith that God is faithful to His promises, giving us what we ask of Him in prayer; and as it is impossible for God to deny Himself, so in like manner is it impossible for Him to break His promises. This faith Our Lord often required of those who asked of Him their health, or the like. To the blind, for instance, He said: "Do you believe that I can do this unto you?" And when they said: "Yea, Lord," He said to them: "According to your faith, be it done unto you. And their eyes were opened." (*Matt.* 9:29-30).

Secondly. This faith produces hope and confidence, on which account St. Paul calls it "the substance of things to be hoped for" (*Heb.* 11:1), because faith in the omnipotence and veracity of God is the strongest pillar and ground of hope, and of all things to be hoped for. For this reason St. Augustine says: "If this faith is gone, prayer is gone with it." (Serm. 36, *De verbo Dom*). It is for this very reason that the Apostle said, when exhorting to prayer: "Whosoever shall call upon the name of the Lord shall be saved" (*Rom.* 10:13); thus giving us to understand that prayer necessarily supposes, not only true faith, but also hope, by a natural consequence, because hope is the nurse of prayer.

As a river will cease to flow if its source be dried up, so, in like manner, there can be no longer any prayer, if its source, that is, hope and confidence, are gone. This confidence was likewise demanded by Jesus Christ, when He said to the man sick of the palsy: "Be of good heart, son, thy sins are forgiven thee" (*Matt.* 9:2); and again, to the woman: "Be of good heart, daughter, thy faith hath made thee whole." (*Matt.* 9:22). From this it is evident that Jesus Christ requires not only faith, but confidence proceeding from faith. Hence St. Thomas Aquinas says: "Prayer derives its efficacy of meriting, from charity; but its efficacy for obtaining, from faith and confidence."

Thirdly. As faith produces hope and confidence, so in like manner do these produce a certain persuasion in the mind that God will grant what we ask of Him. Now the greater the hope and the confidence of the heart, the stronger will be this persuasion in the understanding to obtain the granting of our prayer.

This threefold faith makes prayer efficacious. It is, indeed, a great gift of the Lord to a soul, and almost a certain sign that He will hear her prayer, even though a miracle should be necessary to that effect, should this be for our good, or for the manifestation of the truth, and the glory of the Church. This is that wonder-working faith, that is, faith joined to a firm confidence in God's aid for the working of the miracle. This confidence is produced by an interior impulse of the grace of God, who animates the thaumaturgus (the performer of the miracle), promising him, as it were, His assistance for the miracle which he intends to work. Of this confidence Jesus Christ says: "Amen, I say to you, if you shall have faith and stagger not, not only this of the fig tree shall you do, but also if you shall say to this mountain, Take up and cast thyself into the sea, it shall be done. And all things whatsoever you shall ask in prayer, believing, you shall receive." (*Matt.* 21:21-22).

Now in order to conceive great confidence, to increase it, and to become strengthened and confirmed in it, we must consider what God is in relation to us, and what we are in relation to Him:

First. What is God in relation to us? No one could tell this better than Jesus Christ, His well-beloved Son. "No one," said He, "knoweth the Father, but the Son." (*Luke* 10:22). Now Jesus Christ has told us in distinct language, that "God is our Father." "Thus, therefore, shall you pray: 'Our Father who art in heaven.'" (*Matt.* 6:9). "God is our Father," says Jesus Christ. What we must principally consider in a father is the intense yearning with which he communicates himself and all his goods, as far as possible, to his children. The greater this yearning is, the greater is his charity and liberality.

Now God being our Father, there is in Him an unbounded yearning to communicate Himself. This infinite desire of communicating Himself is essential to God's nature, for God is Infinite Love: love, however, culminates in the reproduction of itself, that is, of generating its own image. Hence faith teaches us that God is Father, and as such, eternally generates another Self, who is His Son, His Most Perfect Image. He, together with His Son, sends forth a third Self, proceeding from Both, who is their reciprocal Love—the Holy Ghost; so that the one and the same Divine Essence is quite the same in each of the three Divine Persons.

But as there can be no multiplication of the infinitely simple Divine Essence, the infinite love which God bears to Himself prompted Him to turn to what is not Himself; that is, to the creation of things, which exist by Him, in Him, through Him, and yet are not Himself. He made them that He might lavish upon them His Perfections to a certain degree. To some of these creatures He gave a rational spirit—to angels and men. Upon them He lavishes His perfections in a more special manner, without ever diminishing Himself in the least, no matter how much He bestows upon them to make them partake of His fullness.

We see clearly the effects of this love, beneficence and communion of God, in the Incarnation of the Divine Word, for the purpose of teaching and saving mankind; we see them in the preaching of Christ, in His Miracles, in His Passion and death; we see them in the Mission of the Holy Ghost; we see these effects in the holy Sacraments, especially in that of the Holy Eucharist, in which God may be said to have exhausted His omnipotence, His wisdom, and His love for man; finally, we see them in His most wonderful care for His Church in general, and for each faithful soul in particular.

Again, in the act of justification, by which God frees the soul from sin and sanctifies her, He communicates Himself not only spiritually to the soul by grace and charity, and other virtues, but He also communicates Himself really, in giving the Holy Ghost. I will dwell more particularly on this point, as I wish to prove my assertion regarding the communicative qualities of God's love. I have said that there is, in God the Father, an infinite desire of communicating Himself and all His goods; I have said that in this love He generated from all eternity

His only-begotten Son. This is, undoubtedly, the greatest act of His infinite charity.

But this Heavenly Father still continues to beget, in time, children who are by grace what the Son of God is by nature, so that our sonship bears the greatest resemblance to the Divine Sonship. Hence St. Paul writes: "Whom he foreknew he also predestined to be made conformable to the image of his Son, that he might be the firstborn amongst many brethren." (*Rom.* 8:29).

Behold, my dear brethren, the great things which Divine love effects! We are the sons of God, as the Holy Scripture says: "Ye are the sons of the living God." (*Osee* 1:107). In this Divine adoption there are infused into the soul not only the grace, the charity, and other gifts of the Holy Ghost, but the Holy Ghost Himself, who is the first and uncreated Gift that God gives to Christians.

In justifying and sanctifying us, God might infuse into our souls His grace and charity to such a degree only as would render us simply just and holy, without adopting us as His children. This grace of simple justification would, no doubt, be in itself a very great gift, it being a participation in the Divine Nature in a very high degree; so that in all truth we could exclaim with the Blessed Virgin: *"Fecit mihi magna, qui potens est*—He that is mighty hath done great things to me."* (*Luke* 1:49).

But to give us only such a degree of grace and participation in His Divine Nature is not enough for the love of God. The grace of adoption is bestowed upon us in so high a degree as to make us really children of God.

But even this measure of the grace of adoption might be bestowed upon us by God in such a manner only as to give by it no more than His charity, grace, and created gifts. This latter grace of adoption would certainly surpass the former, of simple justification, so that, in all truth, we might again exclaim with the Mother of God: *"Fecit po-*

tentiam in brachio suo—He hath showed might in his arm." (*Luke* 1:51).

But neither is this gift, great though it be, great enough for the charity which God bears us. God, in His immense charity for us, wishes to bestow greater things upon us, in order to raise us still higher in grace, and in the participation in His Divine Nature. Hence He goes so far as to give *Himself* to us, so that He might sanctify and adopt us in person.

The Holy Ghost united Himself to His gifts, His grace, and His charity, so that when infusing these gifts into our souls, He infuses, together with them, Himself really in person. On this account St. Paul writes: "The charity of God is poured forth in our hearts by the Holy Ghost, *who is given to us.*" (*Rom.* 5:5). On this very account, the same Apostle calls the Holy Ghost the *Spirit of adoption.* "For you have not received," says he, "the spirit of bondage again in fear; but you have received the *spirit of adoption of children,* whereby we cry: Abba, Father; for the Spirit himself giveth testimony to our spirit, that we are the *children of God;* and if children, heirs also; heirs, indeed, of God, and joint heirs with Christ." (*Rom.* 8:15-17). And: "Whoever are led by the Spirit of God, they are the children of God." (*Gal.* 4:6).

This Divine charity and grace is, no doubt, the height of God's charity for us, and is also, at the same time, the height of our dignity and exaltation, because, on receiving these Divine gifts, we receive, at the same time, the Person of the Holy Ghost, who unites Himself to these gifts, as I have said, and by them lives in us, adopts us, deifies us, and urges us on to the performance of every good work.

Truly, the love and liberality of God effect great things! But even this is not all—we receive still greater favors. In coming personally into the soul, the Holy Ghost is accompanied by the other Divine Persons also, the Father and the Son, from whom He cannot be separated. Therefore, in the act of justification, the three Divine Persons come personally and really into the soul, as into the Temple, living and dwelling therein as long as the soul perseveres in the grace of God. For this reason, St. John writes: "He that abideth in *charity* abideth *in God,* and *God in him*." (*1 John* 4:16). St. Paul writes the same thing: "He who is joined to God is one spirit." (*1 Cor.* 6:17).

Jesus Christ obtained for us this grace, when He prayed on the eve of His Passion: "Holy Father, keep them in thy name, that they all may be one, as thou, Father, in me, and I in thee, that they also may be one in us." (*John* 17:11). Jesus Christ asks of His Father that all His followers might participate in the one and in the same Holy Ghost, so that in Him, and through Him, they might be united to the other Divine Persons. St. Bonaventure says that the just not only receive the gifts, but also the Person, of the Holy Ghost. (*1 Sent. Dist.* 14, a. 2, 9, 1). The same is taught by the renowned Master of Sentences (*Lib. 1,* Dist. 14 & 15), who quotes St. Augustine and others in support of this doctrine. St. Thomas Aquinas asserts the same thing (1, p. 9, 43, a. 3, 6 & 9. 38 Art, 8), and proves that the grace of the Holy Ghost is a peculiar gift, because it is given to all the just. "Grace," says Suarez, "establishes a most perfect friendship between God and man; and such a friendship requires the presence of the Friend, that is, the Holy Ghost, who stays in the soul of His friend, in order to unite Himself most intimately with him, and reside in his soul, as in His Temple, there to be honored, worshipped, and loved."

From what has been said, it follows:

1. That the grace of adoption, or the grace of justification, by which we are sanctified and adopted as the children of God, is something more than a simple quality; it implies several things: the forgiveness of sins, faith,

hope, charity, and other gifts, and even the Holy Ghost Himself, the Author of all gifts, and, as a necessary consequence, the whole Blessed Trinity. All this is infused into the soul in the act of justification, as the Holy Church teaches. (*Concil. Trid.* Sess. 6, chap. 7).

2. It follows that, by this grace of adoption, we are raised to the highest dignity, namely, to the dignity of Divine Sonship, so that, in reality, we are the children of God; yea, even gods, as it were, not only accidentally by grace, but also really by participation in the Divine Nature. Men consider it a great honor to have been adopted by some noble family; but our adoption by God is far nobler, far more honorable. Adopted children receive nothing of the nature of their adoptive father, they inherit only his name and his temporal goods; but we receive from God His grace, and with His grace His Nature. For this reason God is called the Father, not only of Christ, but also of us; because, through grace, He communicates to us His Nature, which he has communicated to Christ by hypostatic union, thus making us the brethren of His Divine Son. St. Paul writes: "Whom he foreknew, he also predestined to be made conformable to the image of his Son, that he might be the firstborn amongst *many brethren*." (*Rom.* 8:29). And St. John says in his Gospel: "He gave them power to be made the sons of God, to them that believe in his name, who are born, not of blood . . . but of God." (*John* 1:12-13).

3. By this grace of adoption we receive an undisputed title to the possession of Heaven.

4. From this grace of adoption, all our works and merits derive their admirable dignity. This adoption of children of God confers upon all our works the greatest dignity and value, making them truly deserving of eternal reward; since they proceed, as it were, from God Himself, and from His Divine Spirit, who lives in us, and urges us on to

the performance of good works.

5. By this grace of adoption, the soul is most intimately united to the Holy Ghost, and thereby elevated far above herself, and, as it were, deified. By thus communicating Himself, God raises the just man, as it were, to a level with Himself, transforming him into Himself, thus making him, as it were, Divine. Love enraptures the loving soul, raises her above her, unites her to the Beloved, and transforms her into Him, so that being, as it were, embodied in Him, she lives, feels, and rejoices in Him alone.

6. This adoption, which commences here below by grace, will be rendered most perfect in Heaven, where we enter upon the possession of God, who will communicate Himself really to our souls, in a manner most intimate and ineffable. On this account St. John says: "Behold the tabernacle of God with men, and he will dwell with them. And they shall be his people: and God himself with them, shall be their God. He that shall overcome shall possess these things, and I will be his God, and he shall be my son." (*Apoc.* 21:3, 7).

This communication and overflow of God's liberality is most wonderful, for five reasons:

First. On account of the greatness and majesty of the Lover and Giver; for who can be greater and more exalted than the Lord of Heaven and earth?

Second. On account of the condition of those to whom He communicates Himself with all His gifts. By nature they are but men, the lowest of rational beings; they are proud, ungrateful, carnal sinners, incapable of doing any good, and prone to every evil; they are mortal, corrupt, vile and disgusting creatures, doomed to become one day the food of worms. "What is man," exclaims the Psalmist, "that thou art mindful of him, or the son of man, that thou visitest him?" (*Ps.* 8:5).

Third. This liberality of God is wonderful on account of

the manifold and extraordinary gifts which He partly confers on men, and partly offers them. These are a rational
soul, created according to God's own Image and Likeness;
His grace; the promise of glory; the protection of His
angels; the whole visible world; and finally, His own well-
beloved Son. "For God so loved the world as to give his
only begotten Son; that whosoever believeth in him might
not perish, but might have life-everlasting." (*John* 3:16).

Fourth. This liberality of God is wonderful, on account
of the end for which He confers all these benefits, that is,
for the happiness of man, and not for His own happiness;
for God does not expect to receive any gain or advantage
from man.

Fifth. On account of the *manner* in which He communicates Himself to men.

1. It is peculiar to God's infinite love to lower Himself
to what is vile and despicable, to heal what is ailing, to
seek what is rejected, to exalt what is humble, and to pour
out His riches where they are most needed.

2. He often communicates Himself even before He is
asked, as He does in all the so-called preventing graces, by
which He moves the soul to pray for subsequent ones.

3. When asked, He always gives more than He is asked
for. The good thief on the cross asked of Jesus Christ no
more than to remember him in His Kingdom; but Jesus
Christ gave him more, saying to him: "Amen I say to thee,
this day thou shalt be with me in paradise." (*Luke* 23:43).

4. God often lavishes His gifts on those who, as He
foresees, will be ungrateful; nay, He lavishes them even
upon the impious, upon infidels, heretics, atheists,
blasphemers, and reprobates, according to what Our Lord
says in the Gospel: "Love your enemies, do good to them
that hate you ... that you may be the children of your
Father who is in heaven, who maketh his sun to rise upon
the good and the bad, and raineth upon the just and the

unjust." (*Matt.* 5:44-45).

Who can, after these reflections, refrain from exclaiming: "Truly, the liberality of God is most wonderful! Who can comprehend its width, its height, its depth? It is fathomless, like the Divinity Itself!"

There are very few who know it to be as great as it has been explained. The holy Apostles and Fathers of the Church never ceased to inculcate it upon the hearts of the Christians. "Behold," exclaims St. John the Apostle, "what manner of charity the Father hath bestowed upon us, that we should be called and should be the sons of God! Dearly beloved, we are now the sons of God. . . . We know that when he shall appear we shall be like to him, because we shall see him as he is." (*1 John* 3:1-2). "Know you not," says St. Paul, "that your members are the temple of the Holy Ghost, who is in you, whom you have from God; and you are not your own, for you are bought with a great price? Glorify and bear God in your body." (*1 Cor.* 6:19-20).

"Our first nativity," says St. Augustine, "is derived from men; our second from God and the Church. Behold, they are born of God. Hence it is that He lives in us. Wonderful change! Admirable charity! For your sake, beloved brethren, the Word was made Flesh; for your sake, He who is the Son of God has become the Son of man, in order that you, from being the children of men, might become the children of God. For out of the children of men He makes the children of God, because though He was the Son of God, He became the Son of man. Behold, how you partake of the Divinity! For the Son of God assumed our human nature that we might become partakers of His Divine nature. By making you participate in His Divinity, He has shown you His charity." (Serm. 24, *De Tempore,* tom. 10).

Another grave author, whilst reflecting upon this immense liberality and charity of God, could not help exclaiming: "The heavens give us light and rain, fire gives us warmth, the air preserves our life, the earth produces various kinds of fruit, the sea gives us fish, animals give us food and clothing; the Eternal Father gives His Divine Nature to His Son; the Father, together with the Son, give their nature to the Holy Ghost; the Son of God gave us Himself in the manger of Bethlehem; He gave us Himself upon the Cross, and He gives us Himself every day, at each Holy Mass, at each Holy Communion. O God! Thou art Almighty; but Thy Omnipotence is not able to give us anything greater in proof of Thy unspeakable love and liberality toward us. I find no better words to express my wonder than those of the saints: 'Lord, Thou hast become foolish from love toward us!'" (*St. Magdalene de Pazzi*). "He has given Heaven, He has given earth; He has given His Kingdom, He has given Himself; what more has He to give? Allow me to say it; how prodigal art Thou of Thyself." (*St. Augustine*).

Who will dare deny, after these considerations, that God is, for us, the best, the kindest, and most liberal of Fathers? Jesus knew this but too well; He knew at the same time, that everyone has most confidence in his own father; He also knew that His heavenly Father wished us to have an unbounded confidence in Him when we pray. Now in order to inspire us with this confidence, He calls our attention to the relation that exists between God and us. He tells us that His heavenly Father is also our Father, whose love, fondness, and promptness to communicate Himself and all His goods to us is infinite. "Amen, amen I say to you, if you ask the *Father any thing* in my name, he will give it to you." (*John* 16:23).

I wish here to call attention to the fact, that, when our Lord Jesus Christ exhorts us to pray, he never uses the expressions: If you ask anything of *"your Creator,"* of *"your*

Lord," of *"your God,"* and the like, He will give it to you. He always says: "If you ask the *Father* anything."

When God exhorts us, in Holy Writ, to be mindful of Him in the days of our youth, He does not say, "Remember thy Father," but "Remember thy *Creator* in the days of thy youth." (*Eccles.* 12:1). Whenever God gave commands to His people He did not say, "Thus saith your Father," but "Thus saith the *Lord*." When God threatened His people to punish them, He did not say, "I, your Father, will visit you with war, famine, pestilence," but He said, "I will visit you with war, famine, pestilence, and then you shall know that I am *your Lord* and *God*."

But whenever our Blessed Lord speaks of prayer, and wishes us to beg for His graces and gifts, He employs the sweet and most amiable name of *Father*. "Thus therefore shall you pray: *Our Father* who art in heaven." (*Matt.* 6:9). And again: "Thou, when thou shalt enter into thy chamber, and having shut the door, pray to thy *Father* in secret; and thy *Father,* who seeth in secret, will repay thee." (*Matt.* 6:6). And again: "Amen, amen I say to you, if you ask the *Father* any thing in my name, he will give it you." (*John* 16:23). "If you then, being evil, know how to give good gifts to your children, how much more will your *Father* who is in heaven give good things to them that ask for them." (*Matt.* 7:11).

Thus Our Lord Jesus Christ teaches us that, when we pray to God, we should not address Him as the *Almighty,* the *Creator,* or the *Saviour,* but we should address Him as our *Father*. The name of Father is most pleasing to God. By calling Him our Father, we give Him more honor than by any other title. According to St. Cyril, "It is something far greater in God to be *Father* than to be Lord; as Father, He generates His Son, who is equal to Himself; but as Lord, He has created the universe, which is infinitely less than Himself." (*Lib. 1, Thesauri,* chap. 6). Oh, how great, then, ought to be your confidence when you pray to your heavenly Father! Were you to ask a favor of some president, or monarch, and should he refer you to your own father, and say, "If he approves of it I will grant it," would you doubt for a moment that you would obtain your request? Oh, how kind is Our Lord! As often as we pray for something, He refers us to His heavenly Father and ours, who is Kindness and Liberality Itself. It is to Him that we are to address our petition, saying, "Abba, Father!" This sweet word touches His heart. Absalom was a degenerate son: he rebelled against King David, his father; and yet, how many and bitter were the tears which David shed when he heard of the death of his son. "The king, therefore, being much moved, went up to the high chamber over the gate, and wept; and as he went, he spoke in this manner: My son Absalom! Absalom, my son! would to God that I might die for thee! Absalom, my son; my son Absalom!" (*2 Kings* 18:33). O holy king! Over whom dost thou weep? Is it not over a rebellious son, who tried to dethrone thee in order to reign in thy place? Shouldst thou, then, not rather rejoice at his death? St. Gregory answers, and says: "Ah, I hear thee answer, 'Thou canst not fathom the love of a father's heart. Absalom, it is true, was an impious son, but he was *my* son; his death causes my heart to bleed, and makes me utterly inconsolable.'"

The Prodigal Son knew very well how guilty he was in the sight of his father; yet remembering the affectionate love of his father's heart, he felt quite consoled, and full of confidence, and said to himself: "I will arise, and will go to my father, and say to him: Father, I have sinned against heaven and before thee." (*Luke* 15:18). "But how can you dare," asks St. Peter Chrysologus, addressing the Prodigal Son, "how can you dare go and see your father, after having caused him so much grief? What hope can you have to be received again into his affections?" "Ah!" answers the Prodigal Son, "he is my father. It is true I have not behaved like a good son, yet, in spite of all that, my father's love for me is not yet dead. His heart will speak for me far more powerfully than I myself can do. As soon as I call him by the endearing name of father, his heart will be moved with compassion; I will go to him without fear." With how great confidence, then, ought not we to pray to our heavenly Father, whom, as Tertullian says, "no one can equal in kindness and liberality." Our heavenly Father says of Himself, speaking by His prophet: "Can a woman forget her infant, so as not to have pity on the son of her womb? And if she should forget, yet will I not forget thee. Behold, I have graven thee in my hands." (*Is.* 49:15-16). Jesus Christ assures us of the same thing, when He says: "And I say not to you that I will ask the Father for you; for the Father himself loveth you." (*John* 16:26-27).

Suppose that your own father were now in Heaven, and that God were to give him unlimited power to grant you whatever you should ask for, with what confidence would you not pray to your own father? Would you doubt in the least that your prayers would be heard? No, you would undoubtedly say, "My father loves me too much to refuse me; I am certain that I shall obtain whatever I ask of him." Now if you have so much confidence in your earthly father, whose love, after all, is but limited, how much greater ought to be your confidence in your heavenly Father, whose power and goodness are unlimited. To doubt, then, of God's goodness, would be to consider Him less merciful than even our own father, which would be rank blasphemy. Far be it from us to make ourselves guilty of such a crime!

If the relation which God bears to us must necessarily inspire us with the greatest possible confidence, the relation which we bear to Him is not less calculated to do so; for if He is our Father, then we are His children, and the laws of all nations, in accordance with those of nature, grant to children a holy right to their father's goods, especially so if these were given him to be transmitted by him to his children.

To illustrate: One day, a poor man called Peter went to his friend Paul, and complained to him of his great poverty. "My dear friend," said Peter, "do you not know anyone who could help me?" "Yes I do," replied Paul; "go to Mr. Bonus, a rich nobleman: he will help you." "I am afraid," said Peter, "he will not receive me." "You need not be afraid," said Paul, "because this nobleman is goodness, liberality, and charity itself; he receives everyone who comes to him with the greatest affability. Some time ago he issued a proclamation, in which he declared that he was the father of the poor, and invited all to come and tell him their wants. He never feels happier than when he bestows alms upon the poor. He is exceedingly rich. He had a dearly beloved son, to whom he bequeathed all his possessions; but his son died a short time after, and on his death-bed willed all his property to the poor, and made his father the executor of his will. Now this good father considers himself bound in conscience to distribute this property to the poor. There is no reason, then, why you should fear to call on him; you will certainly receive what you need." These words filled the heart of Peter with great confidence; he went to see this rich nobleman, and received what he asked for.

Now we are all like the poor man in this parable. We are in want of many things. But we also can have recourse to a Lord who is far more compassionate, and infinitely richer, than the kind-hearted nobleman of whom I have spoken. This good Lord is our heavenly Father. He has issued a proclamation which we find recorded in Holy

Scripture: "Everyone who asketh, receiveth" (*Matt.* 7:8); and, "All things whatsoever you shall ask in prayer, believing, you shall receive." (*Matt.* 21:22). God the Father also has given over everything to His Divine Son Jesus: "All things are delivered up to me by my Father." (*Matt.* 11:27). His Son Jesus died, and made us heirs to all His graces and merits. His heavenly Father considers us as His dear children, who may, in justice, lay claim to the merits and graces of His Divine Son. Our Lord Jesus Christ called our special attention to this right of ours, when He said: "If you ask the Father any thing in *my name,* he will give it to you." (*John* 16:23). He means to say: You must represent to your heavenly Father that He is your Father, and that you are His children, and have as such, according to all Divine and human laws, an indispensable claim upon all His goods. This claim of yours is so much the stronger, as I have acquired it by My Passion and death. It is not on account of your own merits and good works that you are entitled to the gifts and graces of My heavenly Father—it is solely on account of My merits, My sufferings and death, and especially on account of the power which I enjoy with My heavenly Father.

Now if God did not hear us when we pray, we could accuse Him of want of justice toward us, and of want of love toward His Divine Son. But even to think such a thing would be a blasphemy, and utterly unworthy of God. God is, then, bound by His own Divine justice and sanctity to hear and grant our prayers.

During the late war, a Sister of Charity went to an officer of the Union Army to obtain a pass to go south. "Please, sir," said she to the officer, "give me a pass, for the love of God." "I have no love for God," replied the officer. "Give me one, then, for the love of your wife," she asked again. "I have no love for my wife," answered the officer. "Well, then, give me a pass for the love of your children," urged the good sister. "I have no love for my children," was the officer's reply. "Give me one for the love of your best friend."

"I have no such friend," said the officer. "Well," said the sister, "is there nothing in the world that is dear to you, and which you love much? Please reflect a while."

"Oh, yes," said the officer, after a moment's reflection, "I have a dear little child that I love most tenderly." "Well, please then," said the sister, "give me a pass for the love of this dear little child." At these words the officer relented, and gave a pass to the good sister.

Now God bears an infinitely greater love to His beloved Son than this officer did to his child. He is, then, also infinitely more inclined to hear the prayers which we address to Him in the name of His Son. Ah! Pardon me, my God, my heavenly Father, for having compared Thy infinite love for Thy Son to that of an earthly father for his child! What favor and grace canst Thou refuse, if asked in the name of Thy beloved Son? Thou didst hear the prayers of the Jews, when they asked Thee anything in the name of Thy servants Abraham, Isaac, and Jacob; and shall it be said that Thou wilt not hear a Christian who asks of Thee in the name and through the merits of Thy beloved Son? "So great and so powerful is the name of the Son with the Father," says St. John Chrysostom, "that for the sake of this name alone, the Father grants most wonderful gifts." Oh, great, St. John Chrysostom, great indeed is the praise which you bestow upon the power of the name of Jesus! But were you to unite with all the angels and saints of Heaven in describing the power of this holy name, you could not say anything more admirable than what Jesus Christ has said in these few words: "Amen, amen I say to you, *whatsoever* you ask the Father in *my name,* He will give it to you." My Father, says Jesus

Christ, grants *everything—nothing excepted*—that is asked in My name; and in order to take away all doubt from your heart, and make your confidence unwavering, I swear to you: "Amen, amen I say to you, whatsoever you ask the Father in my name, He will give it you." These words, "Amen, amen," are equivalent, in the Hebrew language, to a solemn oath. Who, then, knowing that God has promised so solemnly to hear our prayer, can still harbor the least doubt when he prays in the name of Jesus Christ? Who does not see that such want of confidence would be a great offense against the Omnipotence, the Goodness, and Fidelity of God? No! God, who is infinite Holiness and Justice Itself, cannot deceive us; He will not make a promise unless He intends to fulfill it. Let us, then, say with St. Alphonsus: "As for myself, I never feel greater consolation, nor greater assurance of my salvation, than when I am praying to God and recommending myself to Him. And I think the same must happen to every other Christian. There are several signs by which we can become morally certain of our salvation, but there is none so certain as prayer; for we know with infallible certainty that God will hear him who prays with confidence and perseverance."

Do not say that it is presumption to believe that God is bound to hear our prayers. It would, indeed, be presumption to believe that He was bound to hear us on account of our merits; but it is far from presumption to believe that He is bound to hear us on account of the merits of His Divine Son, on account of His own infinite goodness, and especially on account of the solemn promise He has made to give us whatever we ask in the name of Our Lord Jesus Christ.

Palladius relates that Paul the Hermit one day exorcised a young man who was possessed by an evil spirit. The devil cursed during the entire exorcism, and said:

"Whatever you may do, I shall not leave this young man."
The hermit then commenced to pray to God most confidently: "Why, O Lord, dost Thou not force the devil to
obey me? I have now been praying for half a day, and yet
he will not depart. Now, O Lord, I am resolved neither to
eat nor to drink anything until I see this young man
delivered from the evil spirit." No sooner had the hermit
uttered this prayer, so full of confidence, than the devil
left the young man, howling and blaspheming.

Surius relates that the mother of St. Catherine of Siena
died suddenly, without receiving the last sacraments.
Catherine then began to pray with unusual fervor and
unlimited confidence in God, saying: "Is it thus, O Lord,
that Thou keepest Thy promise, that none of our family
should die an unprovided death? How couldst Thou permit my mother to die without the sacraments? Now, O
Lord, I will not rise from this place until Thou hast
restored my mother to life." And behold, her mother instantly arose from the dead, and lived for several years.

Most wonderful, indeed, is what St. Ananias obtained
by confident prayer. The King of Babylon commanded the
Christians to prove the truth of their religion by causing a
mountain to move from its place; should they not be able
to perform this miracle, they must either renounce their
faith or suffer death. The Christians represented to the
king that it would be a sin to ask a miracle of God merely
to gratify idle curiosity. But the tyrant still insisted. St.
Ananias, Bishop of Jerusalem, hearing of the distress of
the Christians, went to the king, and, full of confidence in
God's promises, said to him: "To show you, O king, that
the promises of the God whom we worship are infallible,
that huge mountain which you see yonder shall not only
move, but it shall even move rapidly." The holy bishop
then said in a loud voice: "In the name of that God who
has promised to him who prays with confidence the power

even to move mountains, I command thee, O mountain, to rise, and move instantly toward the city!" No sooner had the bishop spoken these words than the mountain rose, in the presence of the king and the people, and moved swiftly toward the city, like a vessel sailing before a fair wind. It swept away houses, trees, and everything before it. The king was filled with terror and amazement; and fearing that it would destroy the city, he requested the holy bishop to cause the mountain to stand still. The bishop then prayed, and in an instant the mountain became fixed and immovable as before. (*Petr. de Nat. in Cat. Sanct. 1. 9,* chap. 19).

Let us, then, be assured that God will never refuse a confident prayer. Our hope and confidence are, as it were, the coin with which we can purchase all His graces; He bestows His gifts upon us in proportion to our confidence. God Himself values our confidence exceedingly. We give Him great honor by placing our confidence in Him; for we show thereby that we distrust ourselves, and that we stand in need of His assistance. Whenever we betake ourselves to prayer, let us reanimate our confidence in the Lord; let us imagine to ourselves that we hear the voice of Jesus Christ saying to us: "Whatsoever you ask believing, you shall receive."

Yes, let us pray, but let us pray with confidence for great things, and great things will be given us. Let us pray especially to be delivered from darkness and blindness of the understanding, from attachment to sensual pleasures, from our sins and punishments due to them, and the Lord will deliver us from these evils. Let us pray for a lively faith, for an ardent divine love, and the great gift of confidence in the divine promises, and God will bestow these gifts upon us. "The hand of the Lord is not shortened that it cannot save, neither is his ear heavy that it cannot hear." (*Is.* 59:1). "God is able of the stones to raise up children to Abraham." (*Matt.* 3:9). Can we doubt this truth without being guilty of blasphemy? Oh, the great goodness of God! Did He not change, in a moment, the heart of Saul, and make him, from a persecutor of the Christians, a most zealous defender and propagator of the Gospel? Did not God change the heart of the good thief, of St. Augustine, of St. Mary of Egypt, of St. Margaret of Cortona, and of thousands of other notorious sinners, and make them models of virtue, and ornaments to the Church? Now God will bestow the same graces upon us, if we pray to Him with confidence. "If you, then," says our Divine Redeemer in the Gospel, "being evil, know how to give good gifts to your children, how much more will your Father from heaven give the *good Spirit* to them that ask him?" (*Luke* 11:13). "Hitherto you have not asked anything in my name. Ask and you shall receive, that your joy may be full." (*John* 16:24).

VIII. Our Prayer must be Persevering.

When Holofernes was besieging the city of Bethulia, all men, women, and children began to pray and to fast, crying to the Lord, with tears in their eyes: "Have thou mercy on us, because thou art good." (*Jdt.* 7:20). But as the Lord deferred to come to their aid, they began to despair. Ozias, their leader, rising up all in tears, said: "Be of good courage, my brethren, and let us wait these five days for mercy from the Lord; but if, after five days be past, there comes no aid, we will do the things which you have spoken"; that is, deliver up the city into the hands of the enemy. Now it came to pass that when Judith heard of this, she came and said to them: "What is this word by which Ozias hath consented to give up the city to the Assyrians, if within five days, there come no aid to us? And who are you that tempt the Lord? . . . And you have appointed him a day, according to your pleasure." (*Jdt.*

8:10, 11, 13). Thus Judith reproaches the Jews and their leader for their rashness in having fixed upon the time within which God was to come to their aid. This is not the way to obtain mercy from God, but rather to excite His indignation. "This is not a word that may draw down mercy, but rather that may stir up wrath and enkindle indignation." (*Jdt.* 8:12).

Jesus Christ has, it is true, promised to give us everything we ask of Him, but He has not promised to hear our prayers immediately. The holy Fathers assign many reasons for which He often defers the grant of our petitions:

1. That He may the better try our confidence in Him.

2. That we may long more ardently for His gifts, and hold them in higher esteem. "He defers the granting of them," says St. Augustine, "in order to increase our desire and appreciation of them."

3. "That He may keep us near Him," as St. Francis de Sales says, "and give us occasion to pray with greater fervor and vehemence. He acted thus toward His two disciples at Emmaus, with whom He did not seem willing to stay, before they forced him, as it were, to do so."

4. He delays because, by this means, He wishes to unite Himself more closely to us. "This continual recourse to God in prayer," says St. Alphonsus, "and this confident expectation of the graces which we wish to obtain from God, oh! How great a spur and chain of love are they not to inflame us and to bind us more closely to God!" We must not, therefore, imitate the Jews, by appointing the time within which God is to hear our prayer, as otherwise we would deserve the above reproach of Judith; but let us humble ourselves before the Lord, and pray to Him with tears, that, *according to His will,* so He would show His mercy to us. If we are patient, resigned, and determined to persevere in prayer until He will be pleased to hear us, we

shall not be disappointed in our hope and expectation to receive what we ask of Him.

Our Lord Jesus Christ taught us this when He said: "Ask and you shall receive; seek and you shall find; knock and it shall be opened to you." (*Luke* 11:9). It might seem that He would have said enough by simply saying *"ask,"* and that the words "seek" and "knock" would be superfluous. "But no," says St. Alphonsus, "by them our Saviour gave us to understand that we must imitate the poor when they ask for alms. If they do not receive the alms at once they do not, on that account, cease asking; they return to ask again; and if the master of the house does not show himself they begin to *knock* at the door until they become so troublesome and importunate for him, that he prefers to give them an alms rather than to suffer their importunity any longer." If we pray again and again, in like manner, and do not give up, God will at last open His hands, and give us abundantly. "When thou openest thy hand, they shall all be filled with good." (*Ps.* 103:28).

If men sometimes give alms to poor beggars merely for the sake of ridding themselves of their importunity, "how much more," says St. Augustine, "will our dear Lord give, who both commands us to ask, and is angry if we do not ask." Hence St. Jerome, commenting on the parable of the man who would not give bread to his friend in the middle of the night until he became importunate and annoying in his demands, says: "Not only once, but twice, yea, three times, must we knock, and we must continue to do so until the door of God's mercy be opened." Perseverance is a great thing; if it become importunate, it will prove a better friend to us than the friend mentioned in the parable.

"Let us humbly wait for the consolations of the Lord our God" (*Jdt.* 8:20), and imitate the perseverance of the servants of God in prayer. Moses was a very great servant of the Lord, who would not have granted him a complete victory over the Amalekites had it not been for his per-severance in prayer. "By perseverance in prayer," says St. John Chrysostom (in his sermon on Moses), "he rendered the victory complete." Isaac was very dear to the Lord, and yet, in order to obtain a child, he had to pray for twenty years. "Isaac persevered in praying and sighing to the Lord for twenty years," says the same saint, "and finally he obtained what he asked." (*Hom.* 94, in *Gen.*).

And how did the Lord treat the woman of Canaan? "And behold a woman of Canaan, who came out of those coasts, crying out, and said to him: Have mercy on me, O Lord, thou son of David, my daughter is grievously troubled by a devil." (*Matt.* 15:22). And what does Our Lord reply? He does not so much as even look at her, nor does He give her any answer: "Who answered her not a word." Still she continues to pray with great humility: "Lord, help me." But Our Lord seems not to hear her; so much so, that even his disciples, being annoyed by her in-cessant supplication, "came and besought him, saying: Send her away, for she crieth after us." Instead of hearing her He rejects her like a dog, saying: "It is not good to take the bread of the children and to cast it to the dogs." Who can discover, in this conduct of Our Lord, anything of His usual kindness and condescension which He deigned to show even to the greatest sinners? Will He not, by His manner of acting, intimidate or discourage this woman so as to make her give up all hopes of being heard? But no, Jesus Christ had His wise designs in thus treating her. He knew her faith, and was much pleased with her confidence, which He wished to make shine forth more brilliantly. "But she said: Yea, Lord, for the whelps also eat of the crumbs that fall from the table of their masters." True, indeed, she wished to say, I am but a poor dog; but as such, I beg you to help me, O Lord. And the liberal hand of Jesus opens, and gives her what she wants.

"Then Jesus answering, said to her: O woman, great is thy faith: be it done to thee as thou wilt; and her daughter was cured from that hour." Had this woman been discouraged by the first answer of Our Lord, her daughter would never have been cured.

St. Monica (mother of St. Augustine) was treated in like manner; she had to pray to God for seventeen years before she could obtain of Him the grace of conversion for her son Augustine. Had she become tired with pouring out prayers and shedding tears before the face of the Lord, in all probability the name of Augustine would not now be shining with so great a luster in the calendar of the saints. For twenty years did St. Philip Neri pray for a high degree of the love of God. After that time, this gift was granted him in such a measure as has seldom been granted to man.

Not only were the servants of God, but even Jesus Christ Himself was thus treated by His heavenly Father. Prostrate on His face He prays to Him, but receives neither relief nor comfort. He prays a second time in a most lamentable voice: "Father, if it be possible, let this chalice pass away from me"—neither is He heard this time. He prays a third time with great intensity, and not till then did the angel come to comfort and strengthen Him.

Poor miserable creatures, wretched sinners that we are! How exalted an opinion have we not of ourselves! The heavenly Father lets His only begotten, well beloved, most innocent and afflicted Son, like a poor beggar, knock three times at His door before He opens; and we think we have done enough when we have petitioned a few times at the gate of Heaven! We complain so readily of being unmercifully treated by God, if He does not come at once to our aid, and almost despairing of being heard, we give up praying altogether. "Truly this is not the right way to pray," says St. John Chrysostom; "let us bewail our indolence in praying; for thirty-eight years did the sick man spoken of in the Gospel (*John* 5) wait to be cured, and yet his desire was not fulfilled. Nor did it happen thus through his negligence, yet, for all that, he did not despair; but if we pray for ten days, perhaps, and are not heard, we think it is of no use to pray any longer." (*Homil.* 35, *in Joan*).

We must, then, follow the advice of St. Gregory: "Let us be assiduous in prayer, and importunate in asking: Let us beware of growing remiss in it, when it appears the Lord will not hear us; let us be robbers, as it were, doing violence to Heaven. What robbery can be more meritorious, what violence more glorious? Happy violence, by which God is not offended, but appeased; by which sin is not multiplied, but diminished." (*Comments in Ps.* 129).

If we wish, then, to pray aright, we must not only commence, but must also continue our prayer, especially if we ask something conducive to our own spiritual welfare, or to that of our neighbor. Most men fail in this point, and this is the reason why their prayer is of so little efficacy. Never allow yourself to become guilty of voluntary despondency. "Keep firm to the promise of Jesus Christ," says St. John Chrysostom; "never cease praying until you have received. If you present yourself before the Lord with this firm determination, saying, I will not leave Thee till Thou hast granted my prayer, you will receive most assuredly." (Hom. 24 in *Matt.* 7).

Let us say with the Apostle: "Why should I not be able to do what others have done?" What so many could obtain by their perseverance in prayer, why should we not be able, by our perseverance, to obtain likewise? What a shame will it not be for us to see, on the judgment day, how the saints of Heaven, by their perseverance in prayer, have become what they are; whilst we, for our want of perseverance in prayer, shall appear so very unlike unto them! Most assuredly Almighty God will manifest His power, goodness, and mercy in us, as much as He has done in all the saints, provided we pray for it with the perseverance of the saints.

A priest was once travelling in Scotland. No one could tell that he was a priest. It happened one day, that as he was on his journey, he passed by a house that stood alone in the country. At the moment when he was passing the door, a person came out of the house and asked him if he would come in. The priest did not wish to stop, so he asked what was the matter; why did they wish him to come in. The person at the door answered that the old man of the house was dying; but the old man would not believe that he was dying, although the doctor and everyone had told him that he was dying. The priest then went into the house, and walked upstairs into the room where the old man was. The priest looked at the old man, and saw that he was certainly dying, so he spoke to the old man. "My good man," he said, "you had better get yourself ready for death; you are certainly dying." "Oh, no," answered the old man, "I am sure I shall not die *now*." "But," said the priest, "many deceive themselves about death. They die when they do not think that they are dying. Believe me, for I have seen many die."

"No," answered the old man: "I am quite sure that I shall not die now." "Tell me," said the priest, "what makes you think so?" "I will tell you the truth," said the old man; "I do not know who you are, but I am a Catholic. For thirty years I have prayed every day to God that before I died a priest might come to hear my confession; but there is no priest in this part of the country. After praying to God for thirty years not to die without a priest, God makes me feel sure that I shall not die till a priest comes here." "What you say," said the priest, "is true. If you have prayed to God every day for thirty years not to die without a priest, it is not likely that God will let you die without a priest. I am happy to be able to tell you that a priest is here now: I am a priest." Great was the joy of the old man, and many tears did he shed. Well might he say with the good old man Simeon, "Now, O Lord, thou dost dismiss thy servant according to thy word, in peace; Because my eyes have seen thy salvation." (*Luke* 2:29-30). The old man then made his confession, received the holy Sacraments, and died a very happy death.

Perhaps you might say that it was only by chance that the priest passed the house just when the old man was dying. It is true the priest did not go that way to help the dying man, for he knew nothing about the dying man; but God put it into the mind of the priest to go that way, and to go past that house just at that moment when the old man was dying. God has said, "Ask and it shall be given to you. For everyone that asketh receiveth." (*Matt.* 7:7-8). For thirty years the old man had *asked* of God to receive the Sacraments at his death. So He, who gives to everyone who asks, took care that the Sacraments should be given to him before he died.

So let us pray every day for a happy death. "If we pray for a happy death till the end of our lives, we shall die a happy death." (*Bellarmine*). "You must pray every day for a happy death, and God will grant your prayer every day." (*Suarez*). Pray for a happy death every day when you say, "Holy Mary, Mother of God, pray for us sinners, now *and at the hour of our death*." At holy Mass, and when you receive Holy Communion, pray that you may always be good, and die a happy death.

Chapter 9

HOW TO ACQUIRE THE
SPIRIT OF PRAYER

"I will pour out upon the house of
David, and upon the inhabitants of
Jerusalem, the spirit of grace and of
prayers."—*Zacharias* 12:10.

After having heard so much of the efficacy and advantages of prayer, you must doubtless be desirous to know
how you can acquire that spirit of prayer which the saints
possessed, and which the Lord promised to pour out upon
the inhabitants of Jerusalem. I answer as St. Francis de
Sales did, when asked what one should do to obtain the
love of God: "We must love Him," said he; so, in the same
way, I say, we must pray, in order to learn how to pray.
No art, no trade, no language can be learned without
practice; so, also, prayer cannot be learned without constant exercise. It was only by constant practice that the
saints obtained the spirit of prayer.

St. Teresa was accustomed to offer herself to God fifty
times in the day. St. Martha used to pray a hundred times
in the day, and a hundred times in the night. St. Francis
Borgias, also, was accustomed to pray a hundred times

every day. St. Philip Neri made a kind of rosary of the words: "O God, come to my aid; O Lord, make haste to help me." He recited this rosary sixty-three times in the day, and enjoined on his penitents to do the same. St. Gertrude repeated the prayer: "Thy will be done on earth as it is in Heaven," three hundred and sixty-five times a day. St. Leonard of Port Maurice recommended himself to the Blessed Virgin Mary two hundred times in a day. St. Francis de Sales was accustomed to offer up short and fervent prayers during the day, and thus kept himself in the presence of God, even amidst his many pressing occupations. Blessed Brother Gerard, C.S.S.R., was often beaten by his foreman, who could not bear to see him praying at his work. St. Elizabeth of Hungary was accustomed, in her childhood's days, to steal away from her playmates during their childish sports, and offer up a "Hail Mary." A certain saint never offered up any other form of prayer during thirty years than the simple words: "Lord, have mercy on me!" At the end of this time, the Lord poured out His mercy upon him most abundantly, bestowing on him a high degree of contemplation, and raising him to an eminent sanctity. St. Leonard of Port Maurice used to say that we should not let a moment pass without repeating the words: "Have mercy on me. O Jesus, have mercy on me!" He said that he knew a man who repeated this prayer: "Jesus, have mercy on me!" one hundred times in less than an hour. St. Bartholomew used to offer to God two hundred adorations daily. We read in the Roman Breviary that St. Patrick, when guarding his master's flock, prayed to God a hundred times in the day and a hundred times in the night; and, when a bishop, he daily said the entire Psalter, containing one hundred and fifty Psalms, and many canticles and hymns, besides two hundred other prayers; he also made three hundred genuflections every day, in honor of the Blessed Trinity, and the Sign of the

Cross one hundred times at each canonical hour. Before St. Margaret of Cortona had been raised by God to a high degree of prayer, she was accustomed to pass the time of meditation in reciting the "Our Father." She recited this beautiful prayer as much as a thousand times during the day. She said three hundred "Pater Nosters" in honor of the Blessed Trinity; one hundred in honor of the Blessed Mother of God; one hundred for each of her nearest relations; one hundred in atonement for her sins; one hundred for the Franciscan Order; one hundred for the people of Cortona; one hundred for those who offended her, and many hundred more for the Sovereign Pontiff, for all ecclesiastical Orders, for sinners, heretics, schismatics, Turks, Jews, and heathens.

St. Alphonsus, before going to sleep, used to make the following acts of devotion: ten acts of love; ten acts of confidence; ten acts of sorrow; ten acts of conformity to the will of God; ten acts of love to Jesus Christ; ten acts of love to the Blessed Virgin; ten acts of love to Jesus in the Blessed Sacrament; ten acts of confidence in the Blessed Virgin; ten acts of resignation in suffering; ten acts of abandonment to God; ten acts of abandonment to Jesus Christ; ten acts of abandonment to the Blessed Virgin Mary, and ten petitions to know and do the will of God. Now if this saint made so many acts of devotion before going to sleep, how many must he not have made in the course of the entire day?

But how is it possible, you ask, for one to pray so much in the course of the day? St. Alphonsus himself will answer this question. "Give me," says he, "a soul that truly loves God, and she will know how to do it." For a loving soul to think of her Beloved, and to converse frequently and familiarly with Him, is sweet and agreeable.

But you will say: "I cannot pray as much as the saints have done; in order to do this, I should be a saint myself.

If I cannot acquire the spirit of prayer unless I do as much as they have done, I must give up all hope of ever acquiring it." Softly, my friend; have a little patience! Rome was not built in one day. The saints did not acquire the spirit of prayer all at once; the practice of prayer was not natural to them either, at first; but they persevered in it in spite of every obstacle, and were at last raised to a high degree of contemplation.

The celebrated missionary of Peru, Father Diego Martinez, who converted so many thousands of heathens by his preaching and virtues, lived in constant communion with God; he used to spend whole nights in prayer. Sometimes he was seen raised in the air even above the tops of the highest trees; at such times he appeared surrounded by a heavenly splendor, and kneeling amid two brilliant columns of fire. But he was not satisfied with praying during the night; he prayed, also, during the entire day. As he was constantly occupied with his missionary labors, he maintained the spirit of prayer and recollection by frequent short and fervent ejaculations; these ejaculations often exceeded four thousand, nay, even five thousand, a day. He acquired this wonderful spirit of prayer only by slow degrees. On entering the Novitiate, he resolved to raise his heart to God seven times in the day. After some time he increased this number of ejaculations to one hundred every day, and, before the end of his novitiate, to five hundred. At last this manner of praying became so familiar to him, that the number of his ejaculations amounted to four or five thousand every day.

The saints made use of short and fervent ejaculations as one of the most efficacious means to acquire the spirit of prayer. You, too, will make great progress in this all-important virtue, provided you make use of this means as the saints did—with fervor and perseverance.

But you will ask, "How can I count my ejaculations and

aspirations? It is too troublesome!" I answer, "If you truly love your soul you will soon find out a way to count them, just as well as a merchant knows how to count every cent he spends or receives." In order to do this, you may make use of beads after the example of St. Philip Neri, or you may count your ejaculations on your fingers, or by the hours of the day, making a stated number of them during each hour; for until you have acquired the salutary habit of praying everywhere, it will be advisable for you to count your ejaculations, in order to know whether you may progress in prayer or not.

Should you have resolved to say five times in the day the "Our Father," or "Hail Mary," or "Lord, come to my aid," or "Jesus, have mercy on me," or "Jesus, give me the spirit of prayer," or any other aspiration of the kind, you should be careful to make the number of ejaculations you have imposed on yourself; and as soon as you have acquired a facility in making the proposed number in an hour, raise this number to ten; and, after having succeeded in regularly making ten an hour, increase this number again, and so go on until this manner of prayer has become natural to you, and even a real want of your soul. Should you at first feel no relish in making these ejaculations, continue, nevertheless, and by degrees you will, like the saints, be raised to a higher and more perfect form of prayer and contemplation.

In order to make rapid progress in prayer, you must imitate those who are earnestly engaged in the study of the sciences, or of the fine arts; you will find that such persons lay aside everything that is not connected with the object of their study. To this object are directed all their thoughts and all their efforts, by day and by night. Now if you wish to acquire the spirit of prayer in a short time, you, too, must lay aside everything that could hinder you in acquiring this spirit. Give up useless visits, vain and dangerous amusements. You must bid farewell to the ballroom and the theater; you must cast aside those sentimental novels and silly love stories. If you wish to make rapid progress in the spirit of prayer, you must practice self-denial; you must repress your inordinate inclinations; you must detach your heart from the comforts and pleasures of this life; you must not seek the praise of men, nor desire to do your own will in everything. You must mortify that idle curiosity which prompts you to see and hear everything that passes around you. As long as you do not strive earnestly to detach your heart from everything in this world, you will always have to complain of coldness in prayer, and even of great repugnances to the practices of devotion. You cannot gather grapes from thorns, or figs from thistles. As you sow, so you shall reap. If the wheat which you put into the mill be worthless, so also will the flour which comes from the mill be worthless. Your heart will be where your treasure is, says Our Lord in the Gospel. The devil is well aware of this truth. In order to prevent you from praying, he will place before your mind, when you are engaged in prayer, those objects to which you are most attached.

We have a beautiful example of detachment in the Count Rougemont, of whom St. Vincent de Paul relates the following: "I knew," he says, "in the Province of Bresse, the Chevalier Rougemont, who, in his duels, had wounded and killed an almost incredible number. After his conversion to a very edifying life, I had the pleasure of visiting him at his own residence; he began to speak to me about his devout exercises and practices of virtue, and, among others, of trying to acquire a complete detachment from creatures. 'I feel assured,' said he to me, 'that if I am perfectly detached from creatures, I will be most perfectly united to my Lord and God; for this reason I often examine my conscience to see whether I entertain some attachment, either to myself, or to my relatives, friends, or neighbors; or to the riches and comforts of life, or to any passion or disorderly desire whatsoever that might prevent me from being perfectly united to God, and resting entirely in Him alone. I begin to pray to God to enable me to root out at once whatever I notice to be an obstacle to my perfect union with Him.'

"I remember," continues St. Vincent de Paul, "a remarkable act of this count, which he himself related to me, and which shows how earnestly he went to work to gain a complete detachment from everything; an act which I can never think of without admiration. 'One day,' he said to me, 'I was riding along on horseback; I stopped to make an offering of myself to God; after this I reflected to find out whether there were still something left to which I might have at least some trivial attachment. After having carefully examined all my occupations, recreations, honors, and even the least affections and inclinations of my heart, I found out that I entertained still some affection for the sword which I wore on my side.

"'Why do you wear this sword? I said to myself. But what evil has it done you? Leave it where it is! It has rendered you many great services; it has enabled you to save yourself in thousands of dangers. Should you again be attacked without it, surely you will be lost; but should you fall out again with your neighbor, would you have sufficient self-command to leave it where it is, and not offend God again? My God! What must I do? Shall I still love the instrument of my confusion, and of so many sins? Alas! I see my heart is yet attached to this sword! Now I will not be so mean as to be any longer attached to this miserable instrument! This said, I alighted from my horse, took a stone, and broke my sword into pieces. After this victory over myself I felt completely detached from everything, caring no more for anything in this world, and feeling

most powerfully drawn to love God above all things.'
Behold gentlemen," said St. Vincent, "behold how happy
we should be, and what progress we should make in virtue, if, like this nobleman, we would purify our hearts
from all earthly affections. If our hearts were completely
detached from all creatures, how soon would our souls be
united to God!"

Your facility in prayer, and your attraction for it, will
increase in proportion to the efforts you make to detach
yourself from all earthly things, especially from yourself.
One day Christopher Gonzalve, S.J., a disciple of blessed
Balthazar Alvarez, was asked by one of his fellow students
to tell him by what means he had obtained the extraordinary gift of prayer. He answered: "This did not cost me
very much; I had only to follow the inspiration of God, to
mortify and renounce entirely my desire of vainglory in
scientific matters. I commenced my philosophical studies
with an unusual facility. I gained a great preeminence
over all my companions. This superiority of talent was a
strong lever to ambition, and a source of constant temptation to me. In order to escape these dangerous snares the
more securely, I felt inspired to adopt the following
means, without, however, neglecting my studies: to cause
my companions to lose the high opinion they entertained
of my superior talents, I often asked them an explanation
of certain points which I understood, perhaps, better than
they did. In controversies, I simply gave my opinion, but
appeared to be at a loss how to corroborate it; when objections were made, I answered the first, but for the second I pretended to have no answer. The consequence was
that my professors and fellow students lost the good opinion they had conceived of my talents, and that my professors gave the most difficult and most honorable theses to
others, and to me only such as were very easy, and not
productive of any honor. Now this was exactly what I

desired and aimed at; for I thus gained a complete victory over self-love and ambition, in recompense for which God bestowed upon me the inestimable gift of sublime contemplation, and great familiarity with Him in prayer."

Thus is true what the Lord said by the Prophet Isaias: "If thou turn away thy foot from doing thy own will . . . thou shalt be delighted in the Lord, and I will lift thee up above the high places of the earth, and will feed thee with the inheritance of Jacob, thy Father. For the mouth of the Lord hath spoken it." (*Is.* 58:13-14). Now this promise of the Lord will come true in your regard, also, provided you comply with the conditions, viz.: to purify your heart from all attachment to earthly enjoyments, ambitions, and desires, but especially from all attachment to your own will and judgment. "Yes," says St. Francis de Sales, "God is ready to grant you the gift of prayer, as soon as He sees you empty of your own self-will. If you be very humble, He will not fail to pour it out upon your soul. God will fill your vessel with His ointments, as soon as it is empty of the ointments of this world; that is, as soon as every desire of yours for earthly objects has made room for that of serving and loving Him alone."

The use of frequent and fervent ejaculatory prayers, and the complete detachment of your heart from all creatures, are, it is true, a most powerful means to acquire the spirit of prayer; but in order the most quickly to obtain this inexpressible gift, you must frequently beg it of God; for this grace of prayer is, as St. Francis de Sales assures us, no water of this earth, but of Heaven; therefore you cannot obtain it by any effort of your own, although it be true that you should carefully dispose yourself for the reception of this grace. This care should indeed be great, but humble and calm. You must keep your heart open, waiting for the fall of this heavenly dew; it will fall so much the sooner, the more earnestly and perseveringly you pray and sigh for it every day, especially when you assist at the Divine Sacrifice of Mass, or receive Holy Communion, and visit our most loving Lord in the adorable Sacrament of the Altar. Then you must say to Him: "Lord, teach me how to pray; grant me the spirit of prayer, and a great love for this holy exercise; make me often think of Thee, and find my greatest pleasure and happiness in conversing with Thee; let everything of this world become disgustful to me."

The more frequently and earnestly you make these, or similar petitions, to obtain the spirit of prayer, the more you will receive of this inestimable gift of the Lord, according to the infallible promise of Jesus Christ: "All things whatsoever you ask in prayer, believing, you shall receive." (*Matt.* 21:22). Continue thus asking, until the Lord will accomplish in you what He has promised by the Prophet Zacharias: "I will pour out upon the house of David and upon the inhabitants of Jerusalem the spirit of grace and of prayers." (*Zach.* 12:10). You clearly perceive, from these words of the Prophet, that this gift of prayer is the spirit and gift of the Lord; you must, then, endeavor to obtain it more by asking it of the Lord with great humility, fervor, confidence, and perseverance, than by imprudent efforts of the brain and mind.

Wait patiently for the hour, but do not neglect to do, at the same time, what has been said in this chapter, and then rest assured that the moment will come in which the conversation with God will be easier to you than the conversation with your most intimate friend; and you will exclaim with St. Augustine: "What is more excellent, more profitable, more sublime, and sweeter for the soul, than prayer." You will, with Fathers Sanchez and Suarez, of the Society of Jesus, prefer the loss of all temporal goods to that of one hour of prayer, for then will be realized in you what St. Paul says in his Epistle to the Romans: "The

Spirit also helpeth our infirmity; for we know not what we should pray for as we ought, but the Spirit himself asketh for us with unspeakable groanings." (*Rom.* 8:26). Then the Holy Ghost Himself will pray in you and with you, inspiring such petitions and sighs as are pleasing to and heard by Him. And when the Lord, in His great mercy, has granted you this admirable gift, daily return Him thanks for it, and profit by it, both for your own temporal and spiritual welfare, and that of others.

Say often with the Psalmist: "Take not thy holy spirit from me." (*Ps.* 50:13). Lord, never withdraw from me this spirit of grace and prayer; send me any other punishment for my sins rather than this. I repeat again, never forget to be thankful for this gift, always remembering that you can never fully understand or sufficiently appreciate it until after death. In this gift are included all the gifts and graces of the Lord. Be therefore very desirous to obtain it, and take every possible means to acquire it. You should not take less pains, care and trouble, or make less efforts to obtain this great gift from God, than a good student does to learn a language, an architect to erect a costly and splendid edifice, or a general to gain the victory in an important battle. Would to God you understood this great and inestimable grace as perfectly and clearly as the devil does! I think you would take as much trouble to acquire it, and to preserve it when acquired, as he does to prevent you from receiving it, and to make you lose it when you are in its possession.

This sworn archenemy of our eternal happiness will suffer you to perform any kind of good works, such as fasting, scourging yourself, wearing haircloths, etc., rather than see you striving to advance in prayer; the least time you spend in it is for him an insupportable torment. Although he leaves you quiet at all other times, rest assured that in the time of prayer he will use all his power to distract and disturb you in some way or other. In order to prevent you from praying well, he will fill your mind with thoughts and imaginations of the strangest and most curious kind; so much so, that what you would never think of at any other time will come to your mind at the time of prayer, in such a manner even that it would seem you came to prayer for no other purpose than to be distracted and assaulted by a whole army of the most frightful temptations; or he will make you feel peevish, and try to persuade you that prayer is the business of old women who have nothing else to do, but as for you, that it is only a loss of time, which could be spent much more profitably in some other way.

If you are a priest, a religious, or a student of theology, he will artfully represent to you how necessary and profitable it is to possess great learning, for the salvation of souls and the greater honor and glory of God, in order that the application to study may become your principal occupation, and that you may consider prayer as something merely accessory. If a superior in a conference, a confessor in the confessional, or a priest in a sermon, after the example of Our Lord Jesus Christ, His Apostles, and all the saints, and in accordance with the spirit of the Church, repeatedly insists upon the necessity of prayer, the devil will not be slow to suggest: "Oh, that superior, that priest, knows but one rule, but one obligation; he does not care for science, or consider the country and times in which we are living; if you do what he tells, you will never be anything but a real hypocrite and devotee."

Should this malignant enemy not succeed by these and similar artifices to prevent certain souls from prayer, he will then try other means. To St. Anthony the Hermit, when at prayer, he used to appear in the most hideous forms, to frighten him. He sometimes took St. Frances of Rome, shook her, and threw her on the ground. When St.

Rose of Lima was at prayer, the devil would come and make a great noise, like taking a basket and jumping about with it. He would often cast large hailstones upon the two holy brothers Simplican and Roman, when they knelt down to pray, in order to make them give up prayer, as is related by St. Gregory of Tours.

This implacable hatred and incessant war of Satan against prayer should alone be sufficient to convince you of the necessity, importance, utility and sublimity of this holy exercise; and at the same time urge you on to apply to it with all possible diligence, that you may the sooner acquire the spirit of prayer. Read the life of the seraphic St. Teresa, that great mistress of prayer, and you will find how she struggled for eighteen years to obtain this spirit of prayer. We read of St. Catherine of Bologna, that when she was abbess, one of her daughters, seeing that her whole time was taken up with business, or by the intercourse she was obliged to have with the servants and strangers, asked her how, with her weak health, she could endure so many fatigues and cares. "Know my daughter," replied the holy mother, "and be assured that my mind is so occupied with the things which are not of this world, that at whatever hour or moment I wish, I am immediately united to God and separated from everything bodily and temporal. I confess that this has cost me innumerable sufferings, for the road of virtue is narrow and hard; but, by perseverance, prayer has become my life, my nurse, my mistress, my consolation, my refreshment, my rest, my fortune, all my wealth. It is prayer that has preserved me from mortal sins and rescued me from death; but it has done more than that: It has nourished me as a tender mother nourishes her infant with milk. I ought to add, too, that prayer drives away all distractions and temptations, gives us the desire of doing penance, enkindles in us the divine love, and, finally, that there is no surer road to perfection."

All the saints, were they to come down from Heaven, would, with St. Catherine of Bologna, make the same acknowledgment. The Kingdom of Heaven suffers violence, and those that use this holy violence will bear it away. Let us, like the saints, use this salutary coercion in regard to ourselves; it will prove to us a source of joy for all eternity. Let us, in imitation of the saints, often read a chapter on the great necessity, importance, advantages and efficacy of prayer, thereby to encourage ourselves constantly to persevere and increase in fervent love for this holy occupation. Let us be firmly convinced that such reading will be more profitable to us than any other, whatever it may be. Let us, also, often make our particular examen of conscience on this subject, and let us firmly believe to be true what I one day heard said by a very holy priest, who was so much given to prayer as to be often elevated in the air whilst engaged in devotion: "Anyone," said he, "who would carefully make his particular examen of conscience for half a year, would not fail to attain unto contemplation."

Suppose the Lord would not favor you in prayer as He has favored certain saints, yet be convinced you will always receive far more than you deserve; do what you can, and leave it to Him to do with you according to His will. "He hath filled the hungry with good things," exclaimed the Blessed Virgin Mary. The Lord not only gives, but overloads with His gifts those who have a real desire for them. Join the deed to your desires for them by making use of the means here laid down to acquire them, and rest assured God will deal with you in a most liberal manner, in accordance with the promptness of His paternal heart. You will experience what one of my fellow students has experienced, who said to me one day: "Since I have given myself up to holy prayer, I am quite a different creature." Would to God you did truly relish all that has been said!

If you but knew the gift of God, you would soon see how sweet the Lord is to those who are given up to prayer. You will most assuredly find Him in this holy exercise, for He opens to those who knock, and gives to those who ask. Give it a fair trial. Say with David, "One thing I have asked of the Lord; this will I seek after" (*Ps.* 26:4), viz.: this gift of prayer, and I will ask for it until it shall be granted to me.

Chapter 10

ON THE PRAISES OF PRAYER

As there is nothing more necessary or more profitable to man than prayer, the saints have lavished most profuse eulogies upon this holy exercise. St. John Climachus writes: "Prayer, considered in its nature or quality, is a familiar conversation and union with God; considered in its efficacy, it is the preservation of the world, the reconciliation with God, the mother of tears, the companion on journeys, the propitiation for sins; a bridge over the high waters of temptation; a bulwark against all assaults of afflictions; the suppression and extinction of wars; the office of the angels; the nourishment of all souls; the anticipation of future joy; a perpetual occupation; the source of all virtues; the channel of all graces."*(Gradu. 28, initio).*

Not satisfied with these praises, he adds still greater and more important ones: "Prayer is the lever of the spiritual life; the medicine of the soul; the light of the understanding; the expeller of despair; the ground pillar of Christian hope; the remedy for melancholy and sadness; the riches of monks; the treasure of hermits; the cessation of anger; a mirror to show the progress in the spiritual life; the thermometer of the soul; a declaration of the dispositions of the heart; a moral certainty of heavenly glory."

To these eulogies on prayer may be added the following: "Holy prayer is the column of all virtues; a ladder to God; the support of widows, the foundation of faith; the crown of religious; the sweetness of the married life." (*Auct. Serm. ad. Fratres in eremo apud St. Aug.* Serm. 22). St. Augustine adds: "Prayer is the protection of holy souls; a consolation for the guardian angel; an insupportable torment to the devil; a most acceptable homage to God; the best and most perfect praise for penitents and religious; the greatest honor and glory; the preserver of spiritual health."*(Aug. ad. Probam).*

"Prayer," says St. Ephrem, "is the counter poison of pride; the antidote to the passion of hatred; the best rule in making just laws; the best and most powerful means to govern aright, the standard and trophy in war; a stronghold for peace; the seal of virginity; the guard of nuptial fidelity; the safeguard of travellers; the guardian angel during sleep; the source of fertility for the farmer; a safe harbor in the storms of this life; a city of refuge for criminals; the source of all true joy; the best friend and physician of the dying." (*Tract. de Orat.*). "Prayer," says Cornelius à Lapide, "is the transfiguration of the soul."

Prayer, I add, is, moreover, the paradise of the soul; the Ark of the Covenant; a wonder-working rod of Moses; a pillar of cloud by day and a pillar of fire by night; a *piscina probatica,* or pond of healing water, wherein whoever descends is healed of whatsoever spiritual infirmity he may lie under; an impregnable fortress; the milk of little children; the crosier of bishops; the strength, courage, and persuasive power of missionaries; the conversion of the world; the sanctuary of priests; the wisdom of the saints; the true key of Heaven; the best book of sermons; the mother of good counsel; the school of eloquence; the constancy of the martyrs; the compass of superiors; the interpreter of the Holy Scriptures; the justification for God. If we should say, "I had not sufficient grace to be saved," God will answer: "Why did you not ask it of Me?" Prayer is a kind of soul insurance; and the remembrance of its neglect will be an everlasting torment for the damned, who will see how easily they might have been saved by prayer. "Prayer is," says St. John Climachus, "a pious, gentle tyranny toward God, forcing Him to give up to us everything, even Himself." Hence St. Augustine has said with truth: "What can be more excellent than prayer; what more profitable to our life; what sweeter to our souls; what more sublime, in the course of our whole life, than the practice of prayer!"

Being well convinced of this truth, Caspar Sanchez, S.J., used to say: "Give me all the goods of the earth, and let them last forever, and I will give them all up for half a quarter of an hour of my usual prayer and communion with God." In like manner said Father Francis Suarez, S.J.: "I am willing to lose all my science rather than one hour of prayer." The saintly priest of Ars, named Vianney, used to say: "All the happiness of man on earth consists in prayer." One of our Fathers, a holy man of great experience, often repeated: "Secular people say, 'In the monastery everything is prayer'; but we must reverse their words, and say, 'Prayer is everything to us in the convent.'" Cornelius à Lapide says: "The gift of prayer is an immense and incomprehensible grace of God."

Scarcely did ever any saint, in fewer words, bestow greater praise on prayer than St. Alphonsus, in the preface to his little book on prayer: "I have published several spiritual works, such as *Visits to the Blessed Sacrament; Considerations on the Passion of our Lord Jesus Christ; Glories of Mary;* a work against the materialists and deists, with other devout little treatises; also a little work on the infancy of our Saviour, entitled *Novena for Christmas;* another called *Preparation for Death,* besides the one on the eternal maxims, very useful meditations, or for sermons; to which are added nine discourses, suitable during seasons of divine chastisements, but I am of opinion that I never wrote a more useful book than the present, in which I speak of prayer as a necessary and certain means of obtaining salvation, and all the graces which we require for that object. Would to God it were in my power to give a copy of it to every Catholic in the world, to show him the absolute necessity of prayer for salvation!"

These sentiments of the saints, and of pious souls, proceed from most intimate conviction, and the abundance of the spiritual gifts and graces with which their hearts are overflowing; and it is undoubtedly true that most of men, could they see and comprehend but one-half of the happiness of such souls, would at once give up all earthly pleasures and advantages to enjoy but for one quarter of an hour the happiness of the life of saintly souls. Who, after all this, will remain still cold, careless, and indifferent in the practice of prayer? Most assuredly he only who is *not* of God, and loves darkness more than light; this world more than his soul; the devil, and all his works and pomps, more than the Lord of Heaven and earth.

Chapter 11

ON THE PRACTICE OF MEDITATION

Before entering on the practice and method of meditation, it will be well to establish its necessity. There are two things upon which this necessity is grounded: The first is pointed out by St. Augustine, where he says that he who keeps his eyes shut cannot possibly see either the way or the means of salvation. Eternal truths are spiritual, and cannot be discerned by the eyes of the body, but only by the eyes of the mind in thought and consideration. Now he who does not practice meditation does not consider, and consequently does not see, the importance of eternal salvation, nor the way he should follow to gain it. St. Bernard, writing to Pope Eugenius on this subject, says: "I fear for thee, Eugenius, lest the multitude of affairs, prayer and meditation being intermitted, should bring thee to a hard heart, which docs not dread, because it does not know itself." To obtain salvation we must have tender hearts; that is, docile to receive the impressions of the divine inspirations, and prompt to put them in execution. It was this that Solomon asked for of God: "Give, therefore, to thy servant an understanding heart." (*3 Kgs.* 3:9). It is said in St. John that they who are of God listen to His voice and follow it: "And they shall all be taught of God. Everyone that hath heard of the Father, and hath learned, cometh to me." (*John* 6:45). Our hearts are of themselves hard, because they are wholly inclined to carnal pleasures, and opposed to the laws of the spirit. They are softened by the influx of grace, and this is communicated to them by means of meditation, in which the soul, by considering the divine goodness and the great love which God has for it, and the immense benefits which He has conferred upon it, becomes inflamed, is softened and made obedient to the Divine calls, as David experienced, who said: "In my meditation a fire shall flame out." (*Ps.* 38:4). Without it the heart remains hard, obstinate, disobedient, and will be lost: "A hard heart shall fear evil at the last, and he that loveth danger shall perish in it." (*Ecclus.* 3:27). And remaining hard, it will be so unhappy as not to know that it is so; because the heart which does not meditate "does not dread, because it does not know itself." Because it is sensible of its defects and the impediments which they place in the way of salvation, hence it does not remove them, but soon loves them, and is thus lost.

St. Bernard, be it observed, was writing to a pope who had not, indeed, laid aside meditation (if he even sometimes intermitted it) on account of worldly concerns, but on account of affairs which all regarded the interests of the Church and the glory of God. This should be borne in mind, especially by priests, who, having greater obligations, stand in great need of Divine grace, and consequently of meditation, to obtain strength to discharge them; and not only by those who lay aside meditation to devote themselves to worldly affairs, but by those who neglect it to attend to spiritual works for the good of others, as to hear confessions, preach, or write.

Applicable to this, also, is what St. Teresa (Letter 8) wrote the Bishop of Osma, who, while he attended with great zeal to the salvation of his flock, paid little attention to meditation, from time to time relinquishing it. Hence the saint, having had a particular light, and probably even a revelation of such neglect on the part of this prelate, although he was her director, in order to promote his amendment, did not hesitate to admonish him of it, writing to him as follows: "Representing to Our Lord the graces which He had conferred on your Holiness, in making you humble, charitable, and zealous, I besought Him to give you an increase of all virtues, when He made known to me that your Holiness was wanting in that which is principally necessary (and, if the foundation be wanting, the work cannot stand, but must fall), namely, meditation: not persevering in it with fortitude, and thus interrupting that union, which is the unction of the Holy Spirit, from the want of which arises all that dryness and disunion which the soul experiences." And she adds: "Although it may appear to us that we are free from imperfections, yet, when God opens for us the eyes of the soul, as he is accustomed to do in meditation, we then indeed discover our imperfections." And this, in fact, is what the Holy Ghost declares, that for want of meditation the whole world is filled with sinners, and Hell with souls. "With desolation is all the land made desolate: because there is none that considereth in the heart." (*Jer.* 12:11).

The second fundamental and more weighty principle on which is grounded the necessity of meditation is that those who do not meditate do not pray, and thus lose their souls. The virtues of those who pray cannot be firm and persevering, because perseverance is only to be obtained by prayer, and by persevering prayer. Hence, those who pray not perseveringly will not persevere. It was on this account that St. Paul exhorted his disciples to pray always, without intermission: "Pray without ceasing." (*1 Thess.* 5:17). And for the same reason our Blessed Saviour "spoke a parable . . . that we ought always to pray, and not to faint." (*Luke* 18:1). Meditation, therefore, is morally necessary for the preservation of Divine grace in the soul. I say *morally necessary,* because, although the soul, strictly speaking, may, without the aid of meditation, continue in the state of grace, yet, if meditation be laid aside, it will be morally impossible, that is, very difficult, not to fall into grievous faults; and the reason is, what has just been said, that when a person does not meditate, being distracted with other affairs, he knows but little of his own wants, of his dangers, and of the means which he ought to adopt to escape them, and is but little sensible of the urgent necessity of prayer; and hence he neglects prayer, and by not praying is lost. The great Bishop Palafox, in his annotations of the above mentioned letter of St. Teresa, which he considers one of her most spiritual productions, says: "From this we, as prelates, ought to learn that neither zeal nor charity will suffice without meditation, because virtues unassisted by meditation are deficient, and we shall be lost. The reason is evident: How can charity continue to abide in us if God does not give us perseverance? How will He give us perseverance, if we do not ask it of Him? How shall we ask it of Him without meditation? How can this miracle take place (of obtaining perseverance without meditation), if the channel be wanting through which the Divine influence is conveyed to the soul, which is meditation? Without meditation there is no communication with God for the preservation of virtue; neither is there any other means, nor any other method, of obtaining good things from God."

Our Lord, on the other hand, admonishes us that he who dwells on eternal truths, on death, judgment, and a happy or miserable eternity which await us, will avoid sin: "Remember thy last end, and thou shalt never sin." (*Ecclus.* 7:40). Holy David declared that the consideration of eternity induced him to exercise himself in the practice of virtue, and to correct the imperfections of his soul: "I thought upon the days of old, and I had in my mind the eternal years, and I meditated in the night with my own heart, and I was exercised, and I swept my spirit." (*Ps.* 76:6-7). And if, says a pious author, it were to be asked of the damned, "Why are you now in Hell," the greater part of them would answer: "We are now in Hell because we did not think of Hell." It is impossible that he who calls to mind, in his spiritual exercises, the eternal truths, and attentively dwells upon them and believes them, should not be converted to God. St. Vincent de Paul said that if, during a mission, a sinner should perform all the spiritual exercises, and should not be converted, it would be a miracle, and yet he who preaches and speaks during such exercises is only man; but in meditation it is God who speaks: "I will lead her into solitude, and I will speak to her heart." (*Osee* 2:14).

Assuredly God speaks better and more powerfully than any preacher. All the saints have become saints by means of meditation; and experience shows us that those who practice meditation very seldom fall into mortal sin; and if they unfortunately do sometimes fall into it, they soon arise, by means of meditation, and return again to God. Meditation and sin cannot exist together. A servant of God observes that while many may say the Rosary, the office of the Blessed Virgin, exercise themselves in fasting, and still remain in sin, no one can give himself to meditation and continue an enemy of God; he must either renounce meditation or renounce sin. But if he renounce not meditation, he will renounce not only sin, but all affection to creatures, and give his whole heart to God: "In my meditation a fire shall flame out." (*Ps.* 38:4). Meditation is the furnace in which the soul is inflamed with Divine love. It is impossible to consider attentively the Divine bounty, how much God deserves our love, and the love which He has shown and still shows us, and not be inflamed with His love. The same Royal Prophet says that when he thought of God, and meditated on the wonderful works of His love for man, his heart was inflamed with the most ardent desire to please Him, and his soul rendered incapable of supporting the superabundant consolations with which Our Lord communicated Himself to him: "I remembered God, and was delighted, and was exercised, and my spirit swooned away." (*Ps.* 76:4). We come now to the practice.

The best place for meditation is the church or chapel; but where a person cannot avail himself of these, he may make his meditation at home or in the fields; he may even make it on the road, or at work, by fixing his mind on God. How many poor peasants, having no other opportunities, meditate well while they are at work, or journeying from place to place! He who seeks God finds Him in all places and at all times.

The best time for meditation is the morning. The duties of the day will go on very indifferently if a person neglects to make his meditation in the morning. Meditation ought properly to be made twice in the day, morning and evening; but when it can only be made once, it should be in the morning. The venerable Caraffa says that a fervent act of love, made during the morning meditation, is sufficient to keep the soul in a state of holy fervor during the whole day. As to the length of time which should be spent in meditation, a confessor or director will best regulate that by his experience and prudence. This, however, is certain, that half an hour is not sufficient for those who would attain a high degree of perfection. For those who are only beginning, half an hour may suffice; but, above all, they should not discontinue their meditations when visited by spiritual dryness.

We come now to the different parts of meditation, of which there are three: the preparation, the meditation itself, and the conclusion. The preparation consists of three acts: of faith in the presence of God, of humility, and of prayer for light and assistance. Say for the first: I believe that Thou art present, O God, and I adore Thee from the depth of my own nothingness. For the second: I have deserved Hell, O Lord, on account of my sins; I am sorry for having offended Thee; pardon me, I beseech, in Thy great mercy. For the third: O Eternal Father, for the love of Jesus Christ, and of Mary His Mother, enlighten me in this my meditation, and enable me to profit by it. Then say a "Hail Mary" to the ever blessed Virgin, to obtain this light, and a "Glory be to the Father" to St. Joseph, to your angel guardian, and to your patron saint. These acts should be made attentively, but briefly, and then pass on to the meditation.

For this, those who can read may make use of a book, and pause as soon as anything particularly strikes the mind. St. Francis de Sales says that in this we should imitate bees, which stay on a flower so long as it affords them honey, and then pass on to another. Those who do not know how to read may meditate on the four last things, the benefits and favors of God, and, above all, on the life and Passion of Jesus Christ; which last, St. Francis de Sales says, ought to be the ordinary subject of our meditations. Oh, what a delightful book for devout souls is the Passion of Jesus! In it we may read, better than in any other book, the malice of sin and the love of God for man. The venerable Brother Bernard, of Corlione, having asked our Blessed Saviour if it were pleasing to Him that he should learn to read, the crucifix before which he was kneeling answered: "To read what? What books? I am thy book; this is all that is necessary for thee."

The advantages of meditation consist not only, nor indeed so much, in dwelling seriously on divine truths as in exciting the affections, in praying and resolving: These are the three fruits of meditation. When, then, a person has meditated on some eternal maxim, and when God has spoken to his heart, he must then with his heart speak to God in affections, acts of faith, gratitude, adoration, humility, and above all, love and contrition, which last is also an act of love. Love is the golden bond which binds the soul to God. "Charity is the bond of perfection." (*Col.* 3:14). Every act of love is a treasure in which we are made partakers of the divine friendship: "An infinite treasure to men! which they that use, become the friends of God." (*Wis.* 7:14). "I love them that love me." (*Prov.* 8:17). "He that loveth me, shall be loved of my Father." (*John* 14:21). "Charity covereth a multitude of sins." (*1 Pet.* 4:8).

The venerable Sister Mary of the Cross saw a great fire, in which chaff was consumed as soon as it was thrown into it, by which she was given to understand that, in like manner, all the faults of the soul are done away with and destroyed by an act of Divine love. Moreover, St. Thomas teaches that every act of love acquires for us a degree of eternal glory. Now an act of love is: "My God, I love Thee above all things; I love Thee with my whole heart. I desire that all should love Thee." An act of resignation in all things to the Divine will is: "Make known to me, O Lord, what is pleasing to Thee, and I will willingly accomplish it." An act of oblation of ourselves to God is: "Behold me, and do with me and all things that belong to me what Thou wilt." These oblations of ourselves are so particularly pleasing to God that St. Teresa offered herself to Him fifty times in the day. The most perfect act of love is to delight in the infinite happiness of God. When the soul feels herself united to God by supernatural or infused recollection, she ought not to endeavor to exercise herself in any other acts but those to which she finds herself sweetly inclined by Almighty God, but should lovingly attend to what God works within her, that she may not oppose any obstacle to the Divine operations. If, as St. Francis de Sales advises, in the beginning of her meditation she finds herself inspired by the Holy Spirit with some pious affection, she ought to discontinue reflection, and give herself up to the course of her affections, since the object of meditation is to excite to affections, and hence, the end being obtained, the means should be discontinued.

In the second place, another very great advantage of meditation is its inducing us to pray to God, with humility and confidence, to enlighten us, to pardon us our sins, to grant us perseverance, a happy death, Heaven, and, above all, the gift of His holy love. St. Francis de Sales exhorts us to seek for Divine love before all other graces, because, as he observes, by obtaining love we obtain all. If, however, the soul, on account of spiritual dryness and desolation, cannot exercise herself in this manner, let her repeat that prayer of David: *"Incline unto my aid, O God! O Lord, make haste to help me!"* The venerable Father Paul Segueri said that he had learned from experience that there is no exercise more advantageous in meditation than to pray again and again. We must pray in the name, or through the merits of Jesus Christ, who has promised us, as it has before been said: *"Amen, amen I say to you, if you ask the Father any thing in my name, he will give it to you."*

The third advantage to be derived from meditation is the forming (at least at the end of it) of some good resolution, not only in general, as to avoid all deliberate faults, even the slightest, and to give ourselves wholly to God, but also in particular, as to avoid with greater care some defect to which we may have been more subject, or to practice more diligently some virtue in which we may be called upon to exercise ourselves more frequently, or to bear with the annoyance of some disagreeable person, to obey more exactly a superior or a rule, to be more attentive in mortifying ourselves in some particular circumstances, and the like. We ought never to rise from meditation without making some particular resolution.

The last part of meditation is the conclusion, which should consist of three acts: First, we should thank God for the lights with which He has favored us; secondly, we should resolve to keep our good resolutions; thirdly, we should beseech the Eternal Father, for the love of Jesus and of Mary, to enable us to be faithful to them; and finish all by recommending to Him the souls in Purgatory, the prelates of the Church, sinners, and all our relations, friends, and benefactors, with an "Our Father" and a "Hail Mary," which are the most useful prayers taught us by Jesus Christ and His holy Church.

When we have finished our meditation, we should first, as St. Francis de Sales recommends, make a spiritual nosegay of flowers to smell at the rest of the day; that is, we should select one or two points on which we may have been more particularly affected, and recall them occasionally to our minds, to invigorate us in the discharge of all our duties. Secondly, we should endeavor to put our good resolutions in practice as soon as possible, as well on the trifling as on the great occasions which may present themselves: for example, to overcome with meekness anyone who may be angry with us; or to mortify ourselves in our seeing, hearing, or speaking. And we should be particular in preserving, by means of silence, as far as is possible, the sentiment of those affections which we have experienced; otherwise, if we immediately distract ourselves by useless words or actions, the fervor of devotion which we acquired in our meditation will soon be cooled and extinguished.

Lastly, and above all, we should be constant in meditation, and neither discontinue nor diminish it in time of spiritual dryness, although we should be in ever so great desolation, and that for a long time. How many courtiers, says St. Francis de Sales, come to pay homage to their prince, and are satisfied with being only seen by him! Let us go to meditation to wait on our God and to please Him; and if He be pleased to speak to us, and to favor us with His consolations, let us thank Him for His great goodness; if not, let us be content to remain peaceably in His Divine presence, adoring Him and exposing to Him our wants; and if the Lord should not then speak to us, He will certainly regard our attention and fidelity, and, according to our confidence, will hear our supplications.

THE METHODS OF
CONVERSING CONTINUALLY AND
FAMILIARLY WITH GOD

Taken from the French, with
additions by St. Alphonsus De Liguori.

When holy Job considered that God was so intent on
promoting man's welfare that He desired nothing so much
as to love man and to be loved by man, he wondered; and
addressing himself to Him, exclaimed: "What is a man,
that thou shouldst magnify him? or why dost thou set thy
heart upon him?" (*Job* 7:17). From this it appears that it
is wrong to suppose that to treat with God familiarly and
with great confidence is to be wanting of that respect
which is due to His Divine Majesty. You ought indeed,
devout soul, to reverence Him with all humility, and to
abase yourself before Him, particularly at the remembrance of your ingratitude, and the outrages which you
have committed against Him; but this ought not to hinder
you from treating with Him with the greatest possible love
and confidence. He is Infinite Majesty; but, at the same
time, He is Infinite Bounty and Infinite Love. You have in
God the highest Lord; but you have in Him also the
greatest lover. He does not look down upon you with disdain, but is pleased when you treat with Him with the

201

same confidence, freedom, and love, as children treat with their mothers. Hear how He invites us to present ourselves at His feet, and the caresses which He promises us: "You shall be carried at the breasts; and upon the knees they shall caress you. As one whom the mother caresseth, so will I comfort you." (*Is.* 66:12-13). As a mother delights in taking her child upon her knees, in caressing and feeding him, so does our dear Lord delight in treating with equal love and tenderness those souls who give themselves entirely to Him, and place all their hopes in His goodness and bounty.

First. Reflect that you have neither friend, nor brother, nor father, nor mother, nor spouse, nor lover, who loves you more than God. Divine grace is the rich treasure by means of which we poor servants and most vile creatures become the dear friends of our Creator Himself: "An infinite treasure to men! which they that use become the friends of God." (*Wis.* 7:14). For this end He sought to raise our confidence in Him; *He,* as the apostle expresses it, *emptied Himself,* humbling Himself so as to become man, in order to converse familiarly with us: "Afterwards he was seen upon earth, and conversed with men." (*Bar.* 3:38). He came to become an infant, to become poor, and even to be publicly executed on a cross; He came also to assume the appearances of bread and wine, in order to be our constant companion, and to be intimately united with us: "He that eateth my flesh, and drinketh my blood, abideth in me and I in him." (*John* 6:57). In a word, He loves you as though He had no love but for you alone. And on this account you ought not to love any other but God. Hence you may and ought to say to Him: "My beloved to me, and I to him" (*Cant.* 2:16); my God has given Himself entirely to me, and I give myself entirely to Him; He has chosen me for his beloved, and I choose Him for my only love: "My beloved is white and ruddy, chosen out of thousands." (*Cant.* 58:10).

Second. Say to Him, therefore, frequently: O God, why dost Thou love me so much? What good canst Thou see in me? Hast Thou forgotten the injuries which I have committed against Thee? But since Thou hast dealt with me with such great love, as, instead of consigning me to Hell, to bestow upon me so many graces, whom shall I henceforward love but Thee, who art my only good, my all? My most amiable God, if hitherto I have offended Thee, what most afflicts me now is not so much the punishment which I have deserved, as the displeasure which I have occasioned Thee, who art worthy of infinite love! But Thou knowest not how to despise a heart that repents and humbles itself: "A contrite and humbled heart, O God, thou wilt not despise." (*Ps.* 50:19). How do I now desire, in this life and for the next, no other but Thee! "For what have I in heaven? and besides thee what do I desire upon the earth? . . . Thou art the God of my heart, and the God that is my portion forever." (*Ps.* 72:25-26). Thou alone art and shalt be forever the only Lord of my heart, and of my will; Thou alone my Good, my Happiness, my Hope, my Love, my All. *The God of my heart, and the God that is my portion forever.*

Third. And the more to increase your confidence in God, often call to mind His loving conduct toward you, and the merciful means He has made use of to withdraw you from a disorderly life, from all earthly attachments, and to bring you to His holy love. On these accounts, if you have a determined will to love Him and to please Him as far as you are able, cease to fear Him so as to treat with Him but with little confidence. The mercies which He has shown you are the strongest pledges of His love for you. Diffidence in those who love Him, and whom He loves, is displeasing to Him; so that, if you would be pleasing to His loving heart, treat Him henceforward with the greatest possible confidence and love.

"I have graven thee in my hands; thy walls are always before my eyes." (*Is.* 49:16). My beloved soul, saith Our Lord, of whom art thou afraid and diffident? I hold thee written in My hands, that I may never forget to bestow My benefits upon thee. Art thou afraid of thy enemies? Know that the care of thy defense is always before Me, so that I cannot lose sight of it. For this reason did holy David rejoice, saying: "O Lord, thou hast crowned us as with a shield of thy good will." (*Ps.* 5:13). Who, O God, will be able to hurt us, if Thou defendest us with Thy bounty and love, and with them surroundest us on all sides? Above all, animate yourself to confidence, by considering the gift which God has given us of Jesus Christ. "God so loved the world as to give his only begotten Son." (*John* 3:16). How, exclaims the Apostle, can we ever fear that God will refuse us any good gift, after He has been pleased to bestow upon us even His own Son? "He delivered him up for us all: how hath he not also, with him, given us all things?" (*Rom.* 8:32).

Fourth. "My delights were to be with the children of men." (*Prov.* 8:31). The paradise of God, if so it may be said, is the heart of man. Does God love you? Love Him. His delight is to be with you, and it should be yours to be with Him and to spend the whole time of your life with Him, with whom you hope to spend a blessed eternity.

Fifth. Accustom yourself to speak to Him as though you were alone with Him, familiarly, with confidence and with love, as to your dearest friend, who, of all others, loves you the most. And if it is a great error, as has been said, to treat with God with diffidence, and to wish always to appear in His presence as a timid and bashful slave trembling with alarm before his prince, it would be a still greater error to think that to converse with God is tedious and bitter. No, it is not so: "Her conversation hath no bit-

terness, nor her company any tediousness." (*Wis.* 8:16).
Ask those who really love Him, and they will tell you that
in all the pains and trials of life they can nowhere find
such true and solid consolation as in conversing lovingly
with God.

Sixth. However, a continual application of the mind is
not required of you, so as to neglect your employments
and recreations. Nothing more is required than, without
relinquishing your occupations, to do toward God what
you do on occasions toward those who love you, and
whom you love.

Seventh. Your God is always nigh to you, even within
you: "In him we live, move, and are." (*Acts* 17:28). There
is no screen through which He desires to be spoken to; on
the contrary, He delights in your treating confidently with
Him. Treat with Him of your affairs, of your designs, of
your trials, of your fears, and of whatever concerns you.
Do it above all, as I have said, with confidence, with an
open heart, because God does not usually speak to the
soul that does not speak to Him; since not being accustomed to treat with Him, she would hardly understand
His voice were He to speak to her. And of this Our Lord
complains: "Our sister is little . . . what shall we do to our
sister in the day when she is to be spoken to?" (*Cant.* 8:8).
Our sister is a child in my love; what shall we do by
speaking, if she does not understand me? God would have
us regard Him as our Almighty and most terrible Lord
when we despise His grace, but on the contrary, as our
most loving friend when we love Him; and hence He
desires that we should then speak to Him frequently, in a
familiar manner and without restraint.

Eighth. It is true that God ought always to be treated
with the most sovereign respect; but when He so favors
you as to make you sensible of His presence, and of His
desire that you should speak to Him as to the one who

above all others loves you, express to Him your sentiments freely, and with confidence. "She preventeth them that covet her, so that she first showeth herself unto them." (*Wis.* 6:14). He, without waiting for you to go to Him, when you desire His love, prevents you, and presents Himself to you, bringing with Him the graces and remedies which are necessary for you. He waits only for you to speak to Him, to show you that He is nigh to you, and ready to be united with you, and to console you. "The eyes of the Lord are upon the just; and his ears unto their prayers." (*Ps.* 33:16).

Ninth. Our God, by His immensity, is in all places; but there are two, principally, in which He more specially resides: One is the highest Heaven, where He is present by His glory, which He communicates to the blessed; the other is upon the earth, and is within the humble soul that loves Him: "He dwelleth in the high and holy place, and with a contrite and humble spirit." (*Is.* 57:15). Our God, then, dwelleth in the highest heavens, but disdains not to spend days and nights with His faithful servants in their cells and caves, where He imparts to them His Divine consolations, of which one alone far surpasses all worldly delights, and which He only does not desire who has not experienced them. "O taste, and see that the Lord is sweet." (*Ps.* 33:9)

Tenth. Other friends in this world can converse together only at times, and at others must be separated; but between God and you, if you will, there need never be any separation. "Thou shalt rest and thy sleep shall be sweet . . . for the Lord is at thy side." (*Prov.* 3:24, 26). You may sleep, and God will place Himself at your side, and will watch continually by you. "I shall repose myself with her . . . knowing that she will communicate to me of her good things." (*Wis.* 8:16, 18). When you repose, He departs not from your pillow, but is there ever thinking of you, in order that, when you awake in the night, He may speak to you by His holy inspirations, and receive from you some act of love, of oblation, or of gratitude, thus to keep up with you, even in the hours of rest, His lovely and sweet conversation. And sometimes, even while you sleep, He will speak to you, and will make His voice audible, in order that when you awake you may obey it: "I will speak to him in a dream." (*Num.* 12:6).

Eleventh. He is with you in the morning, to hear from you some word of love or confidence, to be the depository of your first thoughts, and of all the actions which you purpose to perform during the day in order to please Him, as also of all the trials which you offer willingly to undergo for His love and glory. But as He fails not to present Himself to you the moment you awake, do not you fail, on your part, immediately to turn yourself lovingly to Him, and to rejoice at hearing from Him that He is not at a distance from you, as when you were in sin, but that He loves you, and desires to be loved by you, intimating to you at the same moment the lovely precept: "Thou shalt love the Lord thy God with thy whole heart." (*Deut.* 6:5).

Twelfth. Never, therefore, be forgetful of His sweet presence, as are the greater part of men. Speak to Him as frequently as you can; He will not be wearied with you, nor will He, like the lords of the earth, disdain you. If you love Him, you will not be at a loss what to say to Him. Tell Him whatever occurs to you respecting yourself and your affairs, as you would do to a dear friend. Do not regard Him as a haughty prince, who will treat only with the great, and of great things; our God is pleased to abase Himself to treat with us, and is pleased with our communicating to Him our most minute and trivial affairs. He loves you as much, and has as much care of you, as though He had no others to think of but you. He is as much devoted to your interest, as though His providence were to succor only you, His omnipotence to help only you, His mercy and goodness to compassionate only you, to promote your welfare, and to gain, by His endearing ways, your confidence and your love. Freely, therefore, discover to Him the whole of your interior, and beseech Him so to guide you that you may perfectly follow His will, and that all your desires and intentions may be solely directed to please Him, and to gratify His Divine heart: "Bless God at all times; and desire of him to direct thy ways, and that all thy counsels may abide in him." (*Tob.* 4:20).

Thirteenth. Say not, of what use is it to discover all my wants to God? He knows and sees them better than I do myself. He knows them, but He will proceed with you as though He were ignorant of them, if you speak not to Him about them, and crave not His assistance. Our Blessed Saviour was well aware of the death of Lazarus, yet He seemed not to know of it until Mary told Him, when He consoled her by raising her brother to life again.

Fourteenth. Hence, whenever you are afflicted with infirmity, temptation, persecution, or any other trial, betake yourself immediately to Him, and implore His assistance. It will be sufficient for you to represent to Him what it is that afflicts you, saying, "Behold, O Lord, for I am in distress" (*Lam.* 1:20); and He will not delay to console you, or at least to give you strength to bear your trial with patience, which will be of more advantage to you than if He should deliver you from it. Make known to Him all the thoughts which torment you, whether of fear or of sadness, or of any other evil tendency, and say to Him: In Thee, O God, are placed all my hopes; I offer this tribulation to Thee, and I resign myself to Thy will: take pity on me; either deliver me from it, or give me strength to support it. And He will immediately be mindful of the promise which He has recorded in His Gospel, of consoling and comforting all those who in tribulation have recourse to Him: "Come to me all you that labor, and are burdened, and I will refresh you." (*Matt.* 11:28).

Fifteenth. He is not offended when, laboring under afflictions, you seek comfort from your friends, but He would have you have recourse principally to Him. At least, therefore, when you have had recourse to creatures, and they have not been able to console your heart, go to your Creator, and say to Him: Lord, men have only words, they cannot afford me consolation, nor do I any more desire to be consoled by them; Thou alone art my only hope, Thou alone my only love; by Thee alone do I desire to be comforted; and may my consolation be to do, on this occasion, what will be most pleasing to Thee. Behold, I am ready to endure this trial for the whole of my life, and for all eternity, if such should be Thy will, but do Thou assist me.

Sixteenth. Do not be afraid lest He should be offended, if you should sometimes sweetly complain to Him, saying: "Why, O Lord, hast thou retired afar off?" (*Ps.* 9:1). Lord, Thou knowest that I love Thee, and that I desire nothing but Thy love; have pity on me, and help me; do not abandon me. And when desolation continues for a long time, and grievously afflicts you, unite your voice with that of your afflicted and dying Jesus on the Cross, and imploring His pity, say to Him: "My God, my God, why hast thou forsaken me?" (*Matt.* 27:46). Let the thought that, having offended God, you do not deserve His consolation, serve only to humble you the more, and let the conviction that God does, or permits, all for your good, animate you to greater confidence in Him. When you are more than usually troubled and disconsolate, say to Him courageously: "The Lord is my light and my salvation; whom shall I fear?" (*Ps.* 26:1). Thou, O Lord, will enlighten me and save me; in Thee do I confide: "In thee,

O Lord, have I hoped; let me never be confounded." (*Ps.* 30:1). And thus be pacified, knowing that "no one has ever hoped in the Lord and hath been confounded." (*Ecclus.* 2:11). Reflect that your God loves you more than you can love yourself: Of what are you afraid? David consoled himself, saying: "The Lord is careful for me." (*Ps.* 39:18). Say to Him, then: I cast myself into Thine arms, O Lord, and I desire to think only of loving and pleasing Thee. Behold, I am ready to do whatever Thou requirest of me. Thou art not only desirous, but solicitous for my good; to Thee, therefore, do I commit my salvation. In Thee do I rest, and will ever rest, since Thou desirest that I should place all my hopes in Thee: "In peace, in the selfsame, I will sleep and I will rest; for thou, O Lord, hast singularly settled me in hope." (*Ps.* 4:9-10).

Seventeenth. "Think of the Lord in goodness." (*Wis.* 1:1). With these words the wise man exhorts us to have more confidence in the Divine mercy, than fear of the Divine justice; since God is immensely more inclined to bestow favors upon us than to chastise us, as St. James says: "Mercy exalteth itself above judgment." (*James* 2:13). Hence the Apostle St. Peter admonishes us, in our fears for our temporal and eternal interests, to abandon ourselves entirely to the goodness of our God, who takes sovereign care of our salvation: "Casting all your care upon him, for he hath care of you." (*1 Pet.* 7:5). How very applicable to this is the title which David gives to God when he calls Him our God who is ready to save us: "Our God is the God of salvation." (*Ps.* 67:21). This signifies, as Bellarmin explains it, that it is the property of God not, indeed, to condemn, but to save all; for while He threatens those with His displeasure who despise Him, He promises, and hence cannot fail to show, mercy to those who fear Him, according to that of the Blessed Virgin in her Canticle: *His mercy is from generation to generation to them that fear Him.* I place before you, devout soul, all these passages of the Holy Scriptures, that when troubled with doubts whether or not you will be saved, whether or not you are of the number of the predestinate, you may take courage at the thought that you know from God's promises that He desires to save you, if you are resolved to serve and love Him as He requires you.

Eighteenth. When you receive any agreeable news, do not act like some unfaithful and ungrateful souls who, in time of tribulation, have recourse to God, but in time of prosperity forget and forsake Him. Be as faithful to Him as you would be to a loving friend who rejoices in your good; go and communicate to Him your gladness, and praise and thank Him, acknowledging all as coming from His hands; rejoice in your happiness, because it comes to you from His good pleasure, and thus rejoice and be glad solely in Him: "I will rejoice in the Lord, and I will joy in God my Jesus."(*Hab.* 3:18). Say to Him: My Jesus, I bless Thee, and will forever bless Thee for the many favors which Thou hast bestowed upon me, when I deserved from Thee not favors, but punishments, for the offenses which I have committed against Thee. Say to Him with the Sacred Spouse: "All fruits, the new and the old, my beloved, I have kept for Thee." I thank Thee, O Lord, and will ever remember Thy past and present benefits, to honor and glorify Thee for them for all eternity.

Nineteenth. But if you love your God, you ought to rejoice more in Him than in your own happiness. He who has a great love for his friend rejoices more on account of his friend's good than if it were his own. Rejoice, then, in knowing that your God is infinitely happy; frequently say to Him: O Lord, I rejoice more in Thy felicity than in all my own good, because I love Thee more than I love myself.

Twentieth. Another mark of confidence most pleasing to

your most loving God is, when you commit any fault, not to be ashamed to go and cast yourself immediately at His feet, and beg His pardon for it. Think that God is so ready to pardon sinners, that He laments their loss when they depart from Him and die to His grace; and hence He lovingly calls them, saying: "Why will you die, O house of Israel? Return ye and live." (*Ezech.* 18:32). He promises to receive the soul that has forsaken Him as soon as it shall return to His arms: "Turn ye to me ... and I will turn to you." (*Zach.* 1:3). Would that sinners knew with how much compassion Our Lord waits to pardon them! "The Lord waiteth, that he may have mercy on you." (*Is.* 30:18). Would that they were sensible of His desire, not indeed to chastise them, but to see them converted, to embrace and to press them to His heart! He declares: "As I live, saith the Lord God, I desire not the death of the wicked, but that the wicked turn from his way and live." (*Ezech.* 33:11). He adds: "And then come and accuse me, saith the Lord: if your sins be as scarlet, they shall be made white as show." (*Is.* 1:18). As though He had said: Sinners, repent for having offended Me, and then come to Me; if I do not pardon you, *accuse Me,* and treat Me as being unfaithful to My promises: but no, I shall not be wanting to My word; if you come, know that your consciences, though stained as crimson with your crimes, shall, by My grace, be made white as snow.

Twenty-first. In fine, He has said that when the sinner repents for having offended Him, He will forget all his sins: "I will not remember all his iniquities that he hath done." (*Ezech.* 18:22). As soon, then, as you fall into any fault, raise up your eyes to God, make an act of love, and humbly confessing your fault, firmly hope for pardon, saying to Him: "Lord, behold, he whom thou lovest is sick" (*John* 11:3); the heart which Thou lovest is sick, is full of wounds: *Heal my soul, for I have sinned against Thee.*

Thou seekest after penitent sinners; behold, one is at Thy feet, who seeks after Thee; the evil is committed; what must I do? Thou wilt not have me lose confidence; even after the sin which I have committed, Thou desirest my good, and I again love Thee: Yes, my God, I love Thee with all my heart, I am sorry for my sin, and will never more offend Thee; Thou, who art a God *sweet and mild, and plenteous in mercy,* pardon me; let me hear from Thee what Thou didst say to Magdalen: *Thy sins are forgiven thee;* and give me strength, for the future, to be faithful to Thee.

Twenty-second. Then cast your eyes upon Jesus Christ crucified, in order not to be discouraged; offer to the Eternal Father His merits, and confidently hope for pardon. Since to pardon you *He spared not His own Son,* say to Him with confidence: *Look on the face of Thy Christ;* my God, have regard to Thy Son who has died for me, and for His sake grant me pardon. Attend especially, devout soul, to what is commonly taught by masters of a spiritual life, who recommend you to have recourse immediately to God after you have fallen, although you should repeat this a hundred times in the day, and, having done this, not to be any longer disturbed; otherwise, if your soul remain discouraged and troubled on account of the fault which you have committed, it will be able to treat but little with God; it will lose confidence, its desires to love Him will be cooled, and you will be but little able to go forward in the way of the Lord. On the contrary, by having recourse immediately to God, and begging Him to pardon you, promising amendment for the future, your very falls will help you to advance in Divine love. Amongst friends who really love one another it not infrequently happens that, when one offends another and then humbles himself, and asks pardon, their friendship becomes stronger than ever. Do you in like manner, so that your defects may serve to unite you still more closely in love with your God.

Twenty-third. In whatever doubt may occur to you, either concerning yourself or others, as true friends would consult together, so do you never fail to consult God with confidence, and to beseech Him to enlighten you to determine upon what will be most pleasing to Him: "Put thou words in my mouth, and strengthen the resolution in my heart." (*Jdt.* 9:18). O Lord, make known to me what Thou wouldst have me to do or to answer, and I will obey Thy will: *Speak, Lord, for Thy servant heareth.*

Twenty-fourth. Confide in Him so as to recommend to Him not only your own necessities, but those also of others. How pleasing will it be to your God, if, sometimes forgetful of your own interests, you choose to speak to Him of His own glory, of the miseries of others, especially of those who mourn in tribulation, of the souls, His spouses, who are in Purgatory, who sigh to behold Him, and of poor sinners who are deprived of His grace! Say to Him, particularly for these: Lord, Thou art so amiable that Thou art worthy of infinite love; and how canst Thou, then, endure to behold so many souls in the world, upon whom Thou bestowest so many benefits, who desire not to know Thee, nor to love Thee, who even offend Thee and despise Thee! Ah, my most amiable God, cause Thyself to be known, cause Thyself to be loved: *Hallowed be Thy name, Thy kingdom come;* may Thy name be adored and loved by all, and may Thy love reign in the hearts of all. Suffer me not to depart without granting me some grace for the unhappy souls for whom I pray.

Twenty-fifth. It is said that those who in this life have but little longing for Heaven, are punished in Purgatory with a particular suffering, called the pain of languor; and with reason: because to long but little for Heaven is to make but little account of the great happiness of that eternal Kingdom which our Blessed Redeemer purchased for us by His death. Forget not, therefore, devout soul, frequently to sigh after Heaven, saying to your God that your soul longeth and fainteth to see and to love Him face to face. Desire to be liberated from your exile, from this world of sin, and the danger of forfeiting Divine grace, that you may arrive in that land of love where you may love God with all your powers. Say to Him frequently: "So long, O Lord, as I remain upon the earth, I am ever in danger of forsaking Thee and of losing Thy love: When shall I quit this life, in which I so frequently offend Thee? When shall I love Thee with all my soul, and be united with Thee, without the fear of being ever again separated from Thee?" St. Teresa was always sighing in this manner after Heaven; and hence, when she heard the clock strike, she rejoiced at the thought that another hour of life, and of the danger of losing God, was past and gone. She had such a strong desire to die, that she might see God, that she was dying with the desire to die, as she expressed it in the beginning of one of her hymns.

Twenty-sixth. In a word, if you desire to delight the loving heart of your God, be careful, as much as possible, constantly to speak to Him, and with the greatest confidence that He will not disdain to answer you and converse with you. He will not indeed make His voice audible to your corporeal sense of hearing, but very intelligible to your heart, when you withdraw yourself from the conversation of creatures to entertain yourself only with Him: "I will lead her into solitude, and I will speak to her heart." (*Osee* 2:14). He will speak to you by those inspirations, those internal lights, those manifestations of His bounty, those sweet impressions in the heart, those marks of pardon, those feelings of peace, those hopes of Heaven, those interior rejoicings, that sweetness of His grace, those loving embraces—in a word, by those expressions of love which are well understood by those who love, and who seek only Him.

Twenty-seventh. Finally, in order briefly to remind you here of what has been said above, I shall recommend to you a devout practice, by which you may render all your daily actions pleasing to God. When you awake in the morning, let your first thought be to raise up your mind to God, to offer to His honor whatever you may have to do or suffer during the day, and to beseech Him to assist you with His holy grace. Then perform your other morning devotions, making acts of love and of gratitude, and praying, and resolving to spend the day as if it were to be the last of your life.

Father Sanguire recommends making a covenant with God, that, as often as you make a certain sign, such as placing your hand upon your heart, or raising your eyes toward Heaven or to the crucifix and the like, you will thereby intend to make an act of love, of desire to see Him loved by all, of oblation of yourself to Him and the like. When, then, you have made the above-mentioned acts, having placed your soul in the side of Jesus, and under the mantle of Mary, and having besought the Eternal Father, for the love of Jesus and of Mary, to protect you through the day, proceed immediately, before you do anything else, to make your meditation, which should continue for at least half an hour; and let it be your delight principally to dwell on the sorrows, outrages, and sufferings which Jesus Christ endured in His Passion. This, of all subjects, is the most dear to devout souls, and excites them most to the love of God.

Three devotions, above all others, should be your constant practice, if you would improve in a spiritual life: devotion to the Passion of Jesus Christ, to the Blessed Sacrament, and to the ever blessed Virgin. In your meditation make frequent acts of contrition, of the love of God, and of oblation of your whole self to Him. The venerable

Father Charles Caraffa said that a fervent act of the love of God, made in the morning meditation, was sufficient to maintain the soul in fervor throughout the whole day.

Twenty-eighth. Be exact in your other devout practices of going to Confession and Communion, reciting office, etc. When you are about to be employed in external duties, in study, of labor, or any other occupation belonging to your state, at the beginning of every action offer it up to God, beseeching Him to assist you to perform it well, and afterwards frequently retire into the cell of your own heart and unite yourself to God, as St. Catherine of Siena was accustomed to do. In a word, whatever you do, do it with God and for God. When you leave your room, or go out of the house, and when you return, say a "Hail Mary" to recommend yourself to the Blessed Virgin.

When you go to your meals offer to God whatever may be offensive or grateful to your appetite in your eating or drinking; and, after your meals, return Him thanks, saying: "How good indeed art Thou, O Lord, to one who has so much offended Thee!" During the day, give some time to spiritual reading, make a visit to the Blessed Sacrament, and to the most holy Mary; in the evening, recite the Rosary, and make an examination of your conscience, with acts of faith, hope, love, contrition, resolution of amendment, and of receiving during your life, as well as at your death, the Holy Sacraments, with an intention of gaining all the indulgences attached to them. When you go to bed, think that you have deserved to lie in the fire of Hell, and compose yourself to rest in the embraces of the crucifix, saying: *"In peace, in the selfsame, I will sleep and I will rest."*

Twenty-ninth. And here I would incidentally remind you, in a few words, of the many indulgences which are granted for the reciting of certain prayers, or the observance of other devout practices, and of which, in the morning, you should make an intention of gaining as many as you are able. To those who recite the acts of faith, hope, and charity, an indulgence of seven years is granted for each day, and for every month a plenary indulgence, which may also be applied to the souls in Purgatory, and to themselves at the hour of death. Thus, also, direct your attention to the gaining of the indulgences granted for the reciting of the Rosary, with blest rosaries, the Angelus three times a day, the Litany of the Blessed Virgin, the Salve Regina, the "Hail Mary," and the "Glory be to the Father," for saying: "Blessed be the holy and immaculate and most pure Conception of the Blessed Virgin Mary"; as also for saying: "Praise be to the most Blessed Sacrament now and forever"; for the reciting of the prayer "Soul of Christ"; for the bowing of the head at the "Glory be to the Father" and the sacred names of Jesus and Mary; for hearing Mass; for making half an hour's meditation, for which, besides the partial indulgence, there is also a plenary indulgence when continued for a month, with a Confession and Communion during that time; for genuflecting before the Blessed Sacrament, and for kissing the cross. Always have an intention of gaining whatever indulgences are attached to the pious practices which you usually observe.

Thirtieth. In order that you may be able to keep yourself recollected, and in union with God, as far as this life will permit, endeavor, by means of all things which you see or hear, to raise up your mind to God, and to direct your views to eternity. For example, when you see a bubble glide along, think that thus also your life is running on, and that you are approaching to your grave. When you see a lamp going out for want of oil, think that, one day, your life will end in like manner. When you behold tombs, or the bodies of the dead, think that you must become what they are. When you see the great ones of this world rejoicing in honors and riches, pity their folly, and say: "For me my God is my all; some trust in chariots and some in horses, but we will call upon the name of the Lord our God." (*Ps.* 19:8). They may glory in such vain things, but let me glory only in the grace of God, and in His holy love. When you behold pompous funerals, or the magnificent monuments of the great, say: "If their souls be lost, what will all these pomps avail them?" When you look upon the tranquil or stormy sea, consider the difference which there is between a soul in grace and one in the state of mortal sin.

When you see a withered tree, consider a soul devoid of God, which is fit for nothing but to be cast into the fire. If you should ever see a criminal accused of some great crime trembling with shame and fear before his judge, father, or prelate, consider what will be the terror of the sinner before Christ as his Judge. When it thunders, and you are in fear, think of the dread which the damned will forever experience in continually hearing in affliction: "Is there, then, nothing that can prevent my death?" Consider what will be the despair of a soul when it shall be condemned to Hell, and shall exclaim: "Is there, then, nothing that can prevent my eternal ruin?"

Thirty-first. When you see the country, the seacoast, flowers, or fruits, which delight you with their scent or appearance, say: See how many beautiful things God has created for me in this world, in order that I may love Him; and what delights has He not prepared for me in Heaven! St. Teresa said that when she beheld beautiful hills or coasts, they reproached her for her ingratitude to God; and the Abbé de Rancé said that these beautiful works of creation reminded him, and obliged him to love God. St. Augustine said the same, exclaiming: "Heaven and earth, and all things in them, bid me love Thee." It is related of a holy man, that seeing flowers and herbs as he passed through the fields, he was accustomed to strike them with his staff, saying: Be silent: Do not any more reproach me with ingratitude to God; I have heard you, be silent—no more. St. Mary Magdalene de Pazzi, when she held in her hand a fruit or a flower, felt herself excited by it to divine love, saying within herself: Behold, my God has thought from all eternity of creating this fruit, this flower, as a mark of His love toward me.

Thirty-second. When you see rivers or brooks, think that as their waters run toward the sea, and never stand still, so you ought ever to tend toward God, who is your only good. When you are conveyed anywhere by horses, say to yourself: See how these innocent animals fatigue themselves to serve me; and what exertion do I make to serve and to please my God? When you see a dog, for the sake of a miserable bit of bread, so faithful to his master, think how much more faithful you ought to be to God, who has created you, who preserves you, who provides for you, and who loads you with so many benefits. When you hear birds singing, say: My soul, hear how these little creatures praise God their Maker; and what dost thou do? And then praise Him yourself in acts of divine love.

On the contrary, when you hear the cock crow, recollect that you also, like Peter, have denied your God, and renew your sorrow and tears. Thus, also, when you see any house or place in which you have sinned, turn to God and say: "The sins of my youth and my ignorances do not remember, O Lord." (*Ps.* 24:7).

Thirty-third. When you see valleys, consider that as the waters descend into them from the mountains, and fertilize them, so graces from Heaven leave the proud, and descend into the humble and enrich them. When you see a church beautifully adorned, consider the beauty of a soul in grace, which is truly the Temple of God. When you look upon the sea, consider the greatness and immensity of

God. When you see fire or candles lighted on the altar, say: For how many years ought I to have been burning in Hell? But since Thou, O Lord, hast not yet consigned me to that place of woe, grant that my heart may now burn with Thy holy love, even as this fuel or these candles. When you behold the heavens and the stars, say with St. Andrew of Avelino: My feet will one day tread upon those stars.

Thirty-fourth. In order frequently to remind yourself of the mysteries of our Saviour's love for us, when you see hay, a manger, or caves, think of your infant Jesus in the stable of Bethlehem. When you see a saw, or a plane, or a hatchet, remember how Jesus worked as an ordinary youth in the cottage of Nazareth. If you see cords, thorns, nails, or beams of wood, think on the sorrows and death of our Blessed Redeemer. St. Francis of Assisi, when he saw a lamb, was accustomed to shed tears, saying: My dear Lord was led as a lamb to the slaughter to die for me. When you see an altar, chalice, or bread, call to mind the great love which Jesus has shown us in bestowing upon us the most Holy Sacrament of the Eucharist.

Thirty-fifth. Frequently offer yourself to God in the course of the day, as St. Teresa did, saying: Behold me, O Lord; do with me what Thou wilt; make known to me what I must do to please Thee; I desire to do all that Thou requirest of me. Make repeated acts of divine love. The same saint said that acts of love are the fuel which feed and maintain holy love in the soul. When you see any of the brute creation that know not how to love God, and are incapable of loving Him, excite yourself to make more acts of love, seeing that you are capable of loving Him. When you fall into any defect, immediately humble yourself, and with a most fervent act of love endeavor to rise again. When any untoward circumstance happens, immediately offer up the mortification which it occasions you to God, be conformed to His holy will, and accustom yourself on all such occasions to repeat: Thus does God will, thus also do I will. Acts of resignation are acts of love most dear and grateful to the heart of God.

Thirty-sixth. When you are about to resolve upon any undertaking, or to give important advice, recommend yourself to God before you resolve or answer. Repeat as often as you can in the day: *Incline unto my aid, O God! O Lord, make haste to help me!* as St. Rose of Lima was accustomed to do. And for this end turn yourself frequently to the crucifix, or image of the Blessed Virgin, and fail not frequently to invoke the names of Jesus and Mary, especially in time of temptation. God, being Infinite Bounty, has the greatest desire to communicate His graces to us. The venerable Father Alphonsus Alvarez, on one occasion, saw our Blessed Saviour with His hands loaded with graces, going about seeking to whom to dispense them; but He will have us ask Him for them: *ask and you shall receive,* otherwise He will withdraw His hands; on the contrary, He will voluntarily open them to those who invoke Him. And who, says Ecclesiasticus, has ever had recourse to God, and God has despised him and refused to hear him? "Who hath called upon him, and he despised him?" (*Ecclus.* 2:12). And David declares that God showeth not only mercy, but great mercy to those who invoke Him: "For thou, O Lord, art sweet and mild, and plenteous in mercy to all that call upon thee." (*Ps.* 85:5).

Thirty-seventh. Oh, how good and liberal is the Lord to them that lovingly seek Him! "The Lord is good . . . to the soul that seeketh him." (*Lam.* 3:25). He is to be found even by those who do not seek Him. "I was found by them that did not seek me." (*Rom.* 10:20). How much more willingly will He be found by those who do seek Him, in order to love and serve Him?

In fine, St. Teresa says that the souls of the just in this

life have to conform themselves by love to what the blessed do in Heaven. As the saints in Heaven treat only with God, and have no other thought or delight but His glory and love, so must you have no other thought or employment. In this world let God be your only happiness, the only object of your affections, the only end of your actions and wishes, until you arrive in the eternal Kingdom, where your love will be consummated and made perfect, and your desires completely fulfilled and satisfied.

PRAYER TO BE SAID EVERY DAY
TO OBTAIN THE GRACES
NECESSARY FOR SALVATION

BY ST. ALPHONSUS

Eternal Father, Thy Son has promised that Thou wilt grant us all the graces which we ask Thee for in His name. In the name, therefore, and by the merits of Jesus Christ, I ask the following graces for myself and for all mankind:

And first, I pray Thee to give me a lively faith in all that the holy Roman Church teaches me. Enlighten me also, that I may know the vanity of the goods of this world, and the immensity of the Infinite Good that Thou art; make me also see the deformity of the sins I have committed, that I may humble myself and detest them as I ought; and, on the other hand, show me how worthy Thou art, by reason of Thy goodness, that I should love Thee with all my heart. Make me know also the love Thou hast borne me, that from this day forward I may try to be grateful for so much goodness.

Secondly, give me a firm confidence in Thy mercy of receiving the pardon of my sins, holy perseverance, and, finally, the glory of paradise, through the merits of Jesus Christ and the intercession of Mary.

Thirdly, give me a great love toward Thee, which shall detach me from the love of this world and of myself, so that I may love none other but Thee, and that I may neither do nor desire anything else but what is for Thy glory.

Fourthly, I beg of Thee a perfect resignation to Thy will, in accepting with tranquility sorrows, infirmities, contempt, persecutions, aridity of spirit, loss of property, of esteem, of relations, and every other cross which shall come to me from Thy hands. I offer myself entirely to Thee, that thou mayest do with me, and all that belongs to me, what thou pleasest; do Thou only give me light and strength to do Thy will, and, especially at the hour of death, help me to sacrifice my life to Thee with all the affection I am capable of, in union with the sacrifice which Thy Son Jesus Christ made of His life on the cross of Calvary.

Fifthly, I beg of Thee a great sorrow for my sins, which may make me grieve over them as long as I live, and weep for the insults I have offered Thee, the Sovereign Good, who art worthy of infinite love, and who hast loved me so much.

Sixthly, I pray Thee to give me the spirit of true humility and meekness, that I may accept with peace, and even with joy, all the contempt, ingratitude and ill-treatment that I may receive. At the same time I also pray Thee to give me perfect charity, which shall make me wish well to those who have done evil to me, and to do what good I can, at least by praying, for those who have in any way injured me.

Seventhly, I beg of Thee to give me a love for the virtue of holy mortification, by which I may chastise my rebellious senses, and cross my self-love; at the same time I beg Thee to give me holy purity of body, and the grace to resist all bad temptations, by ever having recourse to Thee and Thy most Holy Mother.

Give me grace faithfully to obey my spiritual father and

all my superiors in all things. Give me an upright intention, that in all I desire and do I may seek only Thy glory, and to please Thee alone. Give me a great confidence in the Passion of Jesus Christ, and in the intercession of Mary Immaculate. Give me a great love toward the most Adorable Sacrament of the Altar, and a tender devotion and love to Thy Holy Mother. Give me, I pray Thee, above all, holy perseverance, and the grace always to pray for it, especially in time of temptation and at the hour of death.

Lastly, I recommend to Thee the holy souls in Purgatory, my relations and benefactors; and in an especial manner I recommend to Thee all those who hate me, or who have in any way offended me; I beg of Thee to render them good for the evil they have done, or may wish to do me. I also recommend to Thee all infidels, heretics, and all poor sinners; give them light and strength to deliver themselves from sin. Oh, most loving God, make Thyself known and loved by all, but especially by those who have been more ungrateful to Thee than others, so that by Thy goodness I may come one day to sing Thy mercies in paradise; for my hope is in the merits of Thy Blood, and in the patronage of Mary. O Mary, Mother of God, pray to Jesus for me! So I hope; so may it be!

If you have enjoyed this book, consider making your next selection from among the following . . .

Prices subject to change.

Prices subject to change.

Prices subject to change.

At your Bookdealer or direct from the Publisher.
Call Toll Free 1-800-437-5876

Prices subject to change.